Scotland's :   xit vote has
been positively Nordic – Scots expect diversity and
 mpowerment to be entirely possible – whilst
Westminster's reaction has been decidedly British.
One singer – one song. One deal for everyone – end of.

    ESLEY RIDDOCH

    course, the majority of Nordic nations are EU members.
But perhaps the EEA is a closer fit for Scotland? Perhaps,
     a viable halfway house option would boost support
     cottish independence? Especially since Holyrood
     not automatically retrieve powers from Europe
    t Brexit.

    DDY BORT

McSmörgåsbord

*What post-Brexit Scotland can learn
from the Nordics*

LESLEY RIDDOCH AND PADDY BORT

Luath Press Limited
EDINBURGH
www.luath.co.uk

First published 2017
Reprinted 2017

ISBN: 978-1-912147-00-7

The paper used in this book is recyclable. It is made from
low chlorine pulps produced in a low energy, low emissions manner
from renewable forests.

Printed and bound by
Martins the Printers, Berwick-upon-Tweed

Typeset in 10.5 point Sabon and Solitaire
by 3btype.com

Dedicated to
Eberhard Bort
born 1 December 1954
died 17 February 2017

EBERHARD (PADDY) BORT was the backbone of the Edinburgh
Traditional Music scene and a lynchpin of Nordic Horizons.
Although he came from Germany and spent time in Ireland,
I think the Nordic nations perfectly and unselfconsciously acted
out the 'small is beautiful' mantra at the heart of Paddy's
politics. Paddy was a born-again European – someone who
revelled in the fabulous spectacle of cultural difference without
worry, disapproval or xenophobia and maybe that's why he was
so determined we should produce this book, exploring the vast
array of different relationships between Europe and the Nordic
nations – a palette from which Scotland might soon pick its
own post Brexit relationship. Paddy breathed life into this wee
book from the start and finished all major corrections the day
before he died. It is now dedicated to him and to the small
peaceful Nordic nations he so admired.

Lesley Riddoch

The demographic and economic statistics used in the country boxes in this book were sourced from the following locations:

gov.scot; Scottish Government

mfa.is; Ministry for Foreign Affairs

nrscotland.gov.uk; National Records Scotland

scb.se; Statistics Sweden

ssb.no; Statistics Norway

stat.gl; Grønlands Statistik (Statistics Greenland)

statbank.dk; Statistics Denmark

statbank.hagstova.fo; Statistics Faroe Islands

statice.is; Statistics Iceland

tilastokeskus.fi, pxnet2.stat.fi; Statistics Finland

cia.gov; CIA World Factbook

data.worldbank.org; World Bank

eur-lex.europa.eu; EUR-Lex Access to European Union Law

europa.eu; European Union Official Site

imf.org; International Monetary Fund

and the following publications:

Bache, Ian and Stephen George (2006) *Politics in the European Union*, Oxford University Press. p.540–542

Havemann, Joel (4 June 1992). 'EC Leaders at Sea Over Danish Rejection : Europe: Vote against Maastricht Treaty blocks the march to unity. Expansion plans may also be in jeopardy.' *LA Times*.

Lang, Arabella (14 January 2013). 'Norway's relationship with the EU'. House Of Commons Library.

Contents

Preface

IN STARK CONTRAST to the UK Government's insistence on a 'one singer, one song' approach to Brexit, Nordic experience with the European Union varies dramatically – even within individual Nordic states. The palette ranges from full membership in the case of Finland (in Euro and Schengen) to Sweden (in the EU but outside the Euro), to Denmark (in the EU but outside the Euro, and with the autonomous Faroes and Greenland outside the EU), to Norway (outside the EU but inside the Single Market, and in Schengen) and to Iceland (outside the EU, having dallied with the idea of joining after the banking crash) – and all the Nordic nations square these very varied relationships with Europe with a similar and unchanging membership of the Nordic Council.

This book emerged from an event on 29 October 2016 in Edinburgh, organised by the policy group Nordic Horizons, together with Edinburgh University's Academy of Government, financed by a Scottish Government grant which covered the speakers' travel and accommodation costs. Contributors from the Nordic countries explored their 'Smörgåsbord' of relationships with the EU – and whether Scotland post-Brexit might learn any lessons from their experience. Three hundred people attended, including the Cabinet Secretary for Cultural and External Relations, Fiona Hyslop. It rapidly became clear that Britain is not the only North Atlantic State with mixed views about the EU.

It was good to see Scottish Government ministers meeting the Nordic Horizons speakers – a real Nordic meeting of minds. These small nations have experienced almost every conceivable situation that might befall Scotland – except of course being dragged out of the EU against their will.

We are grateful to Lily Greenan for transcribing the speakers' presentations and to the speakers themselves for their participation and contribution, and thank them for their easy cooperation on this book. We would also like to thank Cabinet Secretary Fiona Hyslop for opening the conference, and the Academy of Government for making it happen at Edinburgh University. Without the grant from the Scottish Government, neither the event nor the book would have been possible. Last, but certainly not least, thanks to Gavin MacDougall and his team at Luath Press.

Nordic Horizons, founded by Nordic policy enthusiast Dan Wynn and journalist, broadcaster and author Lesley Riddoch in 2009, is an informal group of Scottish professionals who want to raise the standard of knowledge and debate about life and policy in the Nordic nations. The Scottish Government has funded Nordic Horizons to bring Nordic experts to Scotland to engage with government officials and other policymakers and influencers. This has led to the development of a Nordic Policy Network within the Scottish Government, where civil servants share information and experiences in order to inform policy.

Lesley Riddoch and Paddy Bort
31 January 2017

The Trading Clubs of Europe, their rules and origins

DEFINITIONS ARE a dull way to start a book. But unless the differences between the EU, EFTA, and EEA are clear from the outset, readers may fail to properly savour the subtle differences in Nordic relations with Europe described in this book. Basically, the EEA is the mechanism that extends the Internal Market of the EU to the three participating states of the European Free Trade Association. EFTA is an alternative trading bloc to the EU created in 1960 with no ambitions for further political integration. Iceland, Liechtenstein and Norway are EFTA members who are also in the EEA (and thus have access to the EU's 500 million consumers.) EFTA's fourth member Switzerland has opted not to join the EEA.

So currently the EEA comprises the 28 EU Member States and the three EEA EFTA States. Simple.

Here's how efta deals with Frequently Asked Questions:[1]

Why was EFTA created and how is it different from the EU?
The European Free Trade Association is an intergovernmental organisation, established in 1960 by the EFTA Convention for the promotion of free trade and economic integration between its member states (today Iceland, Liechtenstein, Norway and Switzerland). EFTA doesn't envisage political integration, it doesn't issue legislation, nor does it establish a customs union.

EFTA's first objective was to liberalise trade between its member states. In 1972, each EFTA State negotiated bilateral free trade agreements (FTAs) with the EEC. Currently, the EFTA States have 26 FTAs in force or awaiting ratification covering 36 partner countries worldwide.

EFTA States are not obliged by the EFTA Convention to conclude preferential trade agreements as a group. They maintain the full right to enter into bilateral third-country arrangements.

1   http://www.efta.int/faq

What is the European Economic Area?

The European Economic Area (EEA) was established by the EEA Agreement in 1994. Its objective is to extend the Internal Market of the EU to the three participating EFTA States, creating a homogeneous European Economic Area. Currently, the EEA comprises the 28 EU Member States and the three EEA EFTA States – Iceland, Liechtenstein and Norway.

Under the present wording of the EEA Agreement, it's impossible to be a party to the EEA Agreement without being a member of either the EU or EFTA.

The EEA Council takes political decisions leading to the amendment of the EEA Agreement, including possible enlargement. Decisions by the EEA Council are taken by consensus between the EU on the one hand and the three EEA EFTA States – Iceland, Liechtenstein and Norway – on the other.

What is covered by the EEA Agreement?

All relevant Internal Market legislation is integrated into the EEA Agreement so that it applies throughout the whole of the EEA. The core of these rules relate to the free movement of goods, capital, services and persons. In addition, the EEA Agreement covers areas such as social policy, consumer protection, environment, company law and statistics. In order to ensure equal conditions of competition throughout the EEA, the EEA Agreement mirrors the competition and state aid rules of the EU Treaties. It also provides for participation in EU programmes such as those for research and education.

What is not covered by the EEA Agreement?

The EEA Agreement does not cover EU common agriculture and fisheries policies, although it contains provisions on farming and fishing trade. The EEA does not have a customs union, common trade policy, common foreign and security policy, justice and home affairs, harmonised taxation or economic and monetary union.

Schengen is not a part of the EEA Agreement. However, all of the four EFTA States participate in Schengen and Dublin through bilateral agreements and they all apply the provisions of the relevant Acquis.

How do the EEA EFTA States contribute financially to the EU?
First, the EEA EFTA States contribute towards reducing economic and social disparities in the EEA through the EEA Grants. Currently the beneficiary states include Bulgaria, Croatia, Cyprus, Czech Republic, Estonia, Greece, Hungary, Latvia, Lithuania, Malta, Poland, Portugal, Romania, Slovakia and Slovenia. In addition to the EEA Grants, Norway has funded a parallel scheme since 2004 – the Norway Grants. The funding period covering 2014–2021 has a total financial envelope of approximately €400 million per year. These contributions are not managed by the EU, but by the EFTA Financial Mechanism Office in collaboration with the beneficiary countries.

Second, the EEA EFTA States contribute towards the EU programmes and agencies that they participate in through the EEA Agreement. These contributions are added to the EU budget, increasing the total financial envelopes of the programmes and agencies in question. For the current 2014–2020 EU multiannual budget period, the total EEA EFTA contribution to EU programmes and agencies is approximately €460 million per year.

Glossary

EEC   European Economic Community, created by the Treaty of Rome, 1957. After the Maastricht Treaty which came into force in 1993, it became the

EC   European Community – one of the three communities (alongside the

ECSC   European Coal and Steel Community of 1951 and

EURATOM   the European Atomic Energy Community of 1957) which were subsumed into the

EU   European Union through the Maastricht Treaty in 1993.

EFTA   European Free Trade Association, an intergovernmental organisation established in 1960 by seven European countries to promote free trade and economic integration to the benefit of its Member States. All original signatories except Norway and Switzerland withdrew from EFTA upon joining what is now the European Union, as did Finland which had become an associate member in 1961 and full member in 1986. As Iceland joined in 1970 and Liechtenstein in 1991 EFTA currently has four Member States: Iceland, Norway, Liechtenstein and Switzerland.

EEA   European Economic Area consists of the 28 Member States of the European Union and three EFTA countries: Iceland, Liechtenstein and Norway, but not Switzerland. The Agreement on the EEA entered into force on 1 January 1994. It seeks to strengthen trade and economic relations between the contracting parties and is principally concerned with the four fundamental pillars of the internal market, namely: the free movement of goods, people, services and capital.

Customs Union

A type of trade bloc in which a group of member countries share a single external trade policy and tariff, though sometimes different import quotas are used. The purpose of a Customs Union is usually to foster increased economic efficiency and closer cultural and political ties between member states. The European Union Customs Union, for example, consists of all EU member countries, as well as Monaco and some UK territories which are not EU members.

Schengen

A group of twenty-six European countries, named for the Schengen Agreement of 1985, which have abolished any type of border or passport control at their shared borders. For the purposes of international travel, the Schengen area functions as a single country with a shared visa policy. Conversely, borders shared with adjacent non Schengen member countries are proportionally stronger.

Brexit

A portmanteau of 'Britain' and 'Exit', the result of a 2016 referendum to determine whether the UK would leave the European Union. 52% of votes were cast in favor of leaving, with Article 50, the clause in European Law that allows member states to withdraw from the Union, set to be triggered in March of 2017.

Timeline

1949

NATO (North Atlantic Treaty Organisation)

Defence Treaty signed initially by 12 countries: by the US and Canada, Belgium, Denmark, France, Iceland, Italy, Luxembourg, the Netherlands, Norway, Portugal, and the United Kingdom. Since then, another 16 states have joined: Greece and Turkey (1952), West Germany (1955), Spain (1982) [East Germany, with German unification in 1990], Hungary, the Czech Republic and Poland (1999), Bulgaria, Estonia, Latvia, Lithuania, Romania, Slovakia and Slovenia (2004), and Albania and Croatia (2009) – so that NATO now comprises 28 states.

1951

European Coal and Steel Community

Treaty of Paris signed by six countries: Belgium, The Netherlands, Luxembourg, France, Germany and Italy.

1957

European Economic Community

The six members of the ECSC sign the Treaty of Rome setting up the EEC and EURATOM, aiming at the creation of a common market, a customs union, plus free movement of capital and labour. EURATOM's goal was the jointly develop nuclear energy.

1960

EFTA

As an alternative to the EEC, the European Free Trade Association emerges, with Austria, Denmark, Norway, Portugal, Sweden, Switzerland and the UK. Like the EEC, EFTA aims to establish free trade, but it opposes uniform external tariffs and sees no need for supranational institutions.

1963

The UK's application to join the EEC is vetoed in 1963, and again in 1967 by Charles de Gaulle.

1968

The EEC's Customs Union is completed.

1972

Norway rejects joining European Community (EEC, ECSC, Euratom).

1973

The UK, the Republic of Ireland and Denmark join the European Community.

1975

UK votes in a referendum by a margin of two-to-one in favour of staying in the EC.

1979

The European Monetary System (EMS) introduces the European Currency Unit (ECU) and the exchange rate mechanism (ERM). All EC members join except the UK.

1981

Greece becomes the EC's tenth member.

1985

Schengen Agreement signed, aiming at a border-free Europe.

1986

Portugal and Spain join the EC, and the European flag is unveiled.

Single European Act (SEA) signed, aiming to complete the formation of a common market.

1992
Maastricht Treaty signed.

1993
Maastricht comes into force, creating the European Union (EU). It paves the way for monetary union and includes a chapter on social policy. The UK negotiates an opt-out on both. The treaty also introduces European citizenship, giving Europeans the right to live and vote in elections in any EU country, and launches European cooperation in foreign affairs, security, asylum and immigration. Denmark had rejected it in a referendum in 1992, but accepted it in 1993 in a second referendum after negotiating an opt-out on monetary union.

1995
Austria, Finland and Sweden join the EU, taking membership to 15. Norway would have joined if voters had not rejected the move in a second referendum in 1994.

Schengen implemented: France, Germany, Portugal, Spain and the Benelux countries are the first to drop border controls except on the EUs external borders – followed later by Austria, Italy, Denmark, Finland, Sweden and Greece, but not the UK or Ireland.

1997
The Amsterdam Treaty is signed, readying the EU for its eastward expansion. More national vetoes are abolished. Laws on employment and discrimination are strengthened, and the social chapter of the Maastricht treaty becomes an

official part of EU law. The Schengen agreement also becomes law, though Ireland and the UK maintain their opt-outs.

2002

Single European Currency, the Euro, is introduced. It had been created in 1999 as the official currency of the then 11 EU countries. Greece adopted the currency two years later, but Sweden, Denmark and the UK stayed out. On 1 January 2002 Euro notes and coins were introduced in the 12 participating states and over the next few months their national currencies were phased out.

2004

Ten countries join the EU: Cyprus, the Czech Republic, Estonia, Hungary, Latvia, Lithuania, Malta, Poland, Slovakia and Slovenia.
New EU Constitution is signed.

2005

Voters in referendums in both France and the Netherlands reject their governments' plans to ratify the EU Constitution. The EU continues on the basis of existing treaties.

2007

Romania and Bulgaria become EU member states.

2009

The Lisbon Treaty, replacing the failed Constitution, extends qualified majority voting, gives more powers to the European Parliament, and provides, for the first time, the possibility of leaving the EU (Article 50).

2013

Accession of Croatia to the EU.

2016

UK referendum on EU membership produces 52: 48 per cent majority for Leave; Scotland votes 62: 38 to Remain.

Scottish Government publishes *Scotland's Place in Europe* setting out proposals for anticipating the impact on Scotland of the UK's exit from the EU.

2017

UK Government publishes *The United Kingdom's exit from, and new partnership with, the European Union* White Paper.

Article 50 to be triggered by UK in March 2017 – to begin the two-year negotiation period with EU.

1

Sampling the Smörgåsbord of Nordic Relations with Europe

LESLEY RIDDOCH AND PADDY BORT

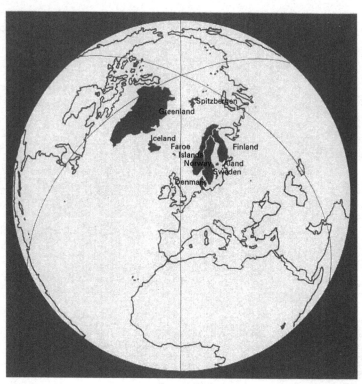

Map of Nordic Nations
The Nordic Council

THE NORDIC NATIONS co-exist quite happily despite having thrashed out every conceivable variation of relationship with the EU. Some are in (Finland, Sweden, Denmark) some are out (Iceland and Norway) and the smallest players have managed to shake it all about (The Faroes and Greenland are out while their 'Mother Ship' Denmark is in). These two tiny Nordic players have a few formal agreements with the EU, whilst Norway pays to retain access to the single market. Denmark is in but its people rejected Euro membership in a referendum, whilst the Finns are all in – members of the EU and the Euro. Surely, among all this kaleidoscopic variation there are lessons for Scotland to learn – as a devolved government within the UK or possibly a small northern independent state sometime in the future.

Another way to characterise this diversity of European relationships is to look at it from west (where fishing limits matter hugely and most Nordic states are outside the EU) to east (where the frontier with Russia /USSR has concentrated minds about the need for European solidarity for decades).

For Greenland, Iceland and the Faroe Islands, fisheries are not just important, they are the defining feature of their economies. Greenland and the Faroe Islands, self-governing parts of EU member Denmark, are outside of the EU because they did not want to become subject to the Common Fisheries Policy. With fishing accounting for 90 per cent of exports from the Faroe Islands, these concerns remain in place. The Faroese used their devolved powers to decide not to follow Denmark into the EEC in 1973; Greenland, which had become a member of the EU when Denmark joined, followed the Faroes after home rule was introduced, with a referendum in 1982 in which 53 per cent voted to leave the EEC – again one of the biggest deciding factors was the Common Fisheries Policy.

For Iceland, too, the EU has been a contentious issue for years. A member of the EEA and EFTA, the barrier to EU membership has been the Common Fisheries Policy – fishing, of course, represents a vital part of the Icelandic economy.

Norway, with its population of just over five million, is in the European Economic Area (EEA) and a member of the European Free Trade Association (EFTA). More than 80 per cent of Norway's exports go to the EU, and more than 60 per cent of imports come from EU countries. Norway decided not to join the European Community in 1972 (in a referendum, 53.5 per cent voted against), and reaffirmed that vote in a second referendum in 1994 (this time, EU membership was rejected by 52.2 per cent). But Norway participates in the Single Market and in Schengen, paying an estimated €9bn as an annual contribution to the EU. Crucially though, it is not part of the common fisheries and common agricultural policies.

Moving east, Denmark, Sweden and Finland, are all less economically dependent on fish and joined the EU to safeguard economic growth within the Single Market, and to promote stability with the EU peace-keeping bloc. The Cold War experience and its long shadow – the presence of the Soviet/Russian frontier loomed larger here – influenced attitudes towards the European Union.

But there are still differences. Denmark is widely regarded as one of the EU's most reluctant players and has voted against EU treaties several times and negotiated four opt-outs. Thus, Denmark is not participating in the common currency and remains exempt from parts of the EU's criminal justice and home affairs system – something it negotiated in 1993. Like Denmark, Sweden has stayed outside the Euro. Only Finland is fully committed to all aspects of EU membership, having been in the Euro from the start.

Reviewing this smörgåsbord of European relationships, where does a post-Brexit Scotland fit in? As we consider our post Brexit options, might we be eyeing up the wrong European prize? Might the halfway house of the European Economic Area (EEA) suit Scotland better than full EU membership? These questions were all posed at the 'Scotland after Brexit' conference in October 2016 when speakers from five Nordic nations explained their very varied outlooks on the same question facing Scotland – is EU membership desirable, oversold or essential? It rapidly became clear that Britain and Scotland were not the only nations with mixed views about the EU.

The Norwegian environmental scientist Duncan Halley explained that in 1992 Norway joined the EEA (essentially the EU's Single Market mechanism) as a precursor to full membership after a referendum in 1994. But fierce debate produced a no vote and the halfway house of the EEA became Norway's permanent home.

Iceland's EEA entry the same year had a slightly different genesis. According to the former Social Democrat leader Jón Baldvin Hannibalsson who masterminded EEA membership, access to the European single market looked like a good way to liberalise a 1960s economy 'more rigid than the Soviet Union.' But because of Iceland's reliance on fishing and relatively recent independence from Denmark, a complete transfer of sovereignty to the EU was not on the cards. 'People said: "We've had 600 years of European colonialism – no more."' It took five years to negotiate the EEA agreement, but it was finally signed, according to Hannibalsson, because an interim solution was mutually beneficial for the EU and small countries like Iceland. The original EFTA – members (The Nordic 4 and the Alpine 3, Austria, Switzerland and Lichtenstein) then conducted more trade with the EU than the USA and Japan combined.

From Iceland's point of view, the combination of EFTA (a rival European trading group) and EEA membership has proved more useful than the full EU deal. EEA members are in the EU's internal market but can opt out of the Common Fisheries or Agriculture Policies, Maastricht, the customs union and the Euro. They can opt in to areas like justice and home affairs and they have free movement in Europe and useful educational and research funds in exchange for a financial contribution.

So might Brexiting Britain aim to join the EEA? Hannibalsson thinks not: 'One, Britain is too big for the EEA; two, its government isn't keen and, three, EU members would have to approve Britain joining the EEA and they are not best pleased with Britain right now.'

It would be a different story for an independent Scotland, he thinks, and maybe – with negotiations and the possibility of a second independence referendum ahead – more feasible.

Opting out of the Common Fisheries Policy (CFP) would not just please Scotland's fishing communities, it could help ensure Scotland's portion of the North Sea becomes as productive and well protected as Norway's portion of the North Atlantic.

Duncan Halley says the Common Fisheries Policy has a terrible record protecting fish stocks in EU waters. Presently 30 per cent of stocks in the North Sea are outside safe biological limits and 93 per cent of cod are fished before they can breed. Meanwhile, according to the OECD, 'stocks in Norway are good,' and 73 per cent of caught fish come from sustainably managed stocks – the highest proportion in the world.

Fishing boats in Norway must be owned by registered fishermen actively working at sea or actively administering boats on land. If Scotland was free to jettison the CFP, it could also end the practice of 'slipper fishing' (where owners of EU quotas trade them and receive income without necessarily actively fishing themselves). Better conservation of stocks could also be achieved if Scots had complete control over Scottish fishing waters – as Iceland, Norway and the Faroes all currently have outside the EU.

Fishing is important in Norway not just because it is valuable – the second biggest export after oil and gas – but because fishing is the backbone of rural Norway, and the industry is of vital importance for continued settlement of the Northern seaboard.

Perhaps Scots should consider such long-term interests before deciding which European club best suits our needs. And perhaps joining a club dominated by small Nordic players (instead of one dominated by large players like Germany and France) could help Scotland shift from a market-dominated, top-down social and economic model towards a more cooperative and decentralised one.

It is important to realise that Nordic states which opt out of the EU are not necessarily anti-European. Far from it. At the Brexit conference, Professor Mary Hilson of Denmark's Aarhus University explained that Nordic cooperation in areas like culture, welfare and the arts flourished during the Cold War while Europe was divided. Proposals for a Scandinavian defence and customs union failed in the 1950s but, since the reunification of Germany created a Baltic dimension in Northern Europe, they are back on the table again. There is even talk of a Nordic Federation, to give those nations a seat at the G20.

Of course, the majority of Nordic nations are EU members. But perhaps the EEA is a closer fit for Scotland than the EU? Perhaps, too, a viable halfway option would boost support for Scottish independence? Especially since Holyrood may not automatically retrieve powers from Europe post Brexit.

Professor Drew Scott, a member of Nicola Sturgeon's Brexit advisory committee, speaking in a personal capacity, said Scotland might not automatically regain powers over fishing, forestry and farming, even though they are devolved. 'Scotland has no international legal identity so the First Minister currently can't sign international agreements – and fishing agreements are most definitely international.' Equally, he suggested, the World Trade Organisation might object if the structure of tariffs was different within a member state, and that could stymy attempts to have a different regime for farming or fishing north of the border within new legislation.

According to Professor Scott,

> There might be a lot to be said for joining the EEA rather than the EU. There's no customs union, so no worry about borders with England should Scotland become independent post Brexit. The EEA won't change in the next five years – the EU most certainly will, and inside the EEA an independent Scotland could straddle two internal markets – the UK and the EEA.

But Duncan Halley isn't sure the limited legal powers of the Scottish First Minister constitute a total stumbling block. He says:

1

Agreements across state boundaries by agencies and local governments are not unusual. Marine Scotland and the Norwegian Fiskeridirektoratet – both the competent authorities in their patches – can, and in each country's individual interest should, coordinate their fish stock management plans. The Scottish and Norwegian governments can decide to stick to their national plans, instructing their competent authorities to administer accordingly. Marine Scotland is instructed by the Scottish Government and not the UK Government. In practice working management to mutual advantage would need no middleman.

On tariffs he observes: 'It's quite right that Scotland cannot vary them, and would need to take them into account in its policy frameworks as with a range of other external factors, such as likely EU tariffs on Scottish products post-Brexit. But that doesn't give the UK Government power to determine anything else regarding internal Scottish systems of fishing or farming/rural support. As the law stands the Scottish Government has full powers to legislate; and indeed has a responsibility to do so as soon as practicable, to have systems ready to replace CAP and CFP.'

The counter argument was made strongly by Tuomas Iso-Markku from the Finnish Institute of International Affairs. He explained why Finland decided, after one year's EEA membership, not just to join the EU but to be at the heart of it, playing a constructive role in every European institution. Like many Nordic policy experts, his biggest criticism of the EEA is that members have full access to the Single Market, but next to no say about the rules that govern it. EU membership, he argues, has given Finland more influence and helped strengthen its identity as a western nation (vitally important given the country's geographical proximity to Russia). He described how 56.9 per cent voted for EU membership, and how quickly a political consensus emerged to place Finland 'close to the core' of the EU, involved 'in all the decision-making.' Finland, he said, wanted to be 'part of the solution, rather than part of the problem.'

Likewise Sweden, which joined the EU in 1995, alongside Finland and Austria. Swedish promoters of EU membership, led by the Social Democrat Ingvar Carlsson and the Conservative leader Carl Bildt, championed Sweden's bid to join because in their view, membership was the only way of avoiding economic decline and a weakening of the welfare state. Since the Cold War had ended, Ingvar Carlsson was able to dismiss worries about independence and sovereignty: 'National politicians have a formal decision-making power over an increasing powerlessness.' Instead, he argued, Sweden could make a positive contribution to the shaping of EU policy and to developing it in a social-democratic direction. In 2003 the Swedes voted to stay outside the Euro by a margin of 56 per cent to 42. But the same exit polls that accurately predicted the Euro result also showed 60 per cent of Swedish voters still favoured basic EU membership.

Although we had two speakers from Denmark, there is no chapter specifically dedicated to Denmark, as Ulrik Pram Gad investigated the case of Greenland, and Mary Hilson helped us to set the scene in a tour d'horizon of the Nordic countries. During the British Brexit referendum campaign, Denmark was one of the countries mentioned regularly as the most likely country to follow the British example – to have a referendum on EU membership and potentially leave the club. After all, the Danes joined along with the Brits in 1973, and have since been close allies of the UK (often voting with the UK in the Council of Ministers). Denmark's traditional Euroscepticism seemed to make it the prime candidate in the domino theory of Brexiteers as the next member to fall. That was backed by the political climate in Denmark in recent years, with centre-right and centre-left parties coming under increasing pressure from the highly-Eurosceptic Danish People's Party (DPP). The DPP has forced the more moderate liberals, conservatives and Social Democrats to swing towards a more authoritative Eurosceptic agenda – underlined by Morten Messerschmidt's record result as the DPP lead candidate in the 2014 European Parliament elections.

In the run-up to the UK referendum, a series of Danish polls showed substantial support in Denmark for a similar poll – 40 per cent were in favour of a referendum, while 45 per cent were against (these surveys also suggested, though, that a majority of Danes preferred to stay in the EU). Nonetheless, the DPP renewed its calls for a vote over Denmark's membership of the EU in the wake of the Brexit vote. The DPP's Marie Krarup even dismissed Russia as the country's main threat and instead pointed the finger at the EU. And the left-wing Red-Green Alliance (RGA) has also echoed the call for a EU referendum.

Even though polls in Denmark (after the British vote for Leave), actually showed support for a referendum had fallen to 32 per cent and support for remaining in the EU had soared to 69 per cent.

EU-friendly sentiments have had proven strength in other polls too, as Professor Marlene Wind, the Director of the Centre for European Politics at the University of Copenhagen, observed:

> In a post-Brexit referendum survey asking whether people fully support EU membership, 70 per cent of Danish voters answered positively. The same tendency has been apparent in Sweden and the Netherlands. Contrary to what was predicted by many doomsayers, few European voters have been won over by the Brexiteers' victory. A Eurobarometer poll published in July suggests that the free movement of people, goods and services is viewed as the most positive result of the EU, and no country other than Britain

registered less than 68 per cent support for the principle of freedom of movement. In Denmark, this continued support for the EU has meant the Unity List – the country's most left-wing party – is now alone in making a rather lacklustre request for a Danish referendum.[1]

In Finland, a poll following the UK's Brexit vote found more than 69 per cent of Finns were not in favour of holding such a vote.

So which Nordic state does Scotland most strongly resemble?

Like Finland we are in bed with an elephant (to borrow Ludovic Kennedy's famous phrase – borrowed in turn from Pierre Trudeau who coined it for Canada and the US in 1969) and maybe like Russia's tiny Nordic neighbour, our choices are more limited by the proximity of England than we think.

Scotland has different economic interests to the fishing-led economies of the North Atlantic, closer proximity to Europe and a history of EU membership. There is also a difference in outlook between EFTA and the EU. EFTA prides itself on espousing market liberalism, while the EU has a much more comprehensive agenda. It may also seem politically unwise to rock the boat by offering a different vision of Scotland's future in Europe to the one so recently supported by 62 per cent in the Brexit referendum. But a mature democracy takes the long view – and, that might be EEA membership for an independent Scotland as a first or even a permanent halfway house.

This book explores the way neighbouring Nordic nations have resolved trading and political dilemmas similar to those currently facing Scotland.

---

1   Marlene Wind, '"Dexit" off the table as Danish Euroscepticism abates', Europe's World, 7 November 2016, Autumn 2016; <http://europesworld.org/2016/11/07/dexit-off-table-danish-euroscepticism-abates/#.WI9fJSidBHg>.

2

Norden – an intertwined history

MARY HILSON

Organisation	Denmark	Finland	Iceland	Norway	Sweden	Greenland	Faroes
CoE	Yes	Yes	Yes	Yes	Yes	Yes	Yes
EEA	Yes	Yes	Yes	Yes	Yes	No	No
EU	Yes	Yes	No	No	Yes	No	No
Eurozone	No	Yes	No	No	No	No	No
NATO	Yes	No	Yes	Yes	No	Yes	Yes
OECD	Yes	Yes	Yes	Yes	Yes	Yes	Yes
UN	Yes	Yes	Yes	Yes	Yes	No	No
WTO	Yes	Yes	Yes	Yes	Yes	No	No

COE	Council of Europe
EEA	European Economic Area
EU	European Union
Eurozone	countries sharing the common Euro currency
NATO	North Atlantic Treaty Organisation
OECD	Organisation for Economic Co-operation and Development
UN	United Nations
WTO	World Trade Organisation

2

MARY HILSON is one of the most respected British academics writing on the Nordic nations – though she now lives and works in Denmark. She grew up outside the EU in Guernsey – a childhood experience of life beyond the EU that might stand her in good stead now as she waits to discover if Brexit will force her to seek a residence permit to continue in her permanent post as Professor of History at Aarhus University.

Mary's interest in Scandinavia was kindled by accident, when she had the chance to go to Uppsala University in Sweden as an exchange student while studying Economic and Political Development at Exeter University.

At that point, in 1992, Sweden was not a member of the EC and Mary had to apply for a residence permit:

2

I got there just as the financial crisis hit. It was a time of enormous political and social change in Sweden but I wasn't really aware of that. I lived in a student flat with other exchange students. All we knew was that life in Sweden was very expensive. I enjoyed the courses I took in Swedish politics and economic history and became interested in the Swedish system of government and the welfare state – but I was unaware that much of what I was studying was changing rapidly before my very eyes.

Mary's PhD was on British labour history, which brought her back to Sweden as a point of comparison. 'I had the language skills to be able to read the sources.' It seems that experience informed much of her later interest in the wider Nordic model(s) which led to her classic book of the same name.[1] Mary started writing whilst she was teaching at the Department of Scandinavian Studies, University College London, and finished the book in Helsinki. One amazon reviewer wrote:

I had long wondered whether the Scandinavian political model is as successful as it is often perceived to be, and if so, why it has succeeded there and run into problems in so many other regions. This book went a long way to helping me answer these questions. I personally found the author's explanation of the vastly different origins of the Scandinavian and other socialist movements to be very revealing. The former, she explains, owes much to the gradual formation of mutually beneficial cooperatives out of a mosaic of small agricultural land holdings whereas British socialism arose primarily as a response to exploitation of the labour force.

Mary also took evening classes in Finnish while she was at UCL – one of the few universities in the UK that teaches the rather difficult language and offers degree programmes covering modern and medieval Nordic history, literature and culture. So, is she more at home in Britain or in Denmark?

---

1   Mary Hilson, *The Nordic Model: Scandinavia since 1945*, London: Reaktion Books, 2008.

On a personal level Denmark is home:

My partner has got a job here too so we are finally working in the same place, for the first time since 1998. The move over here in the summer of 2015 was so easy. I registered with the International Citizen Service in Aarhus – it was a piece of cake. But it was a summer when tens of thousands of people were moving across borders and so it was sobering to realise how easy it was for me compared to Syrian refugees trying to reach Germany and Denmark. I've no idea yet what the future holds regarding my situation here. Nothing has happened yet but Danish citizenship rules are quite strict – among other things you must live here for nine years to apply for citizenship.

Mary's thoughts on the sudden explosion of interest in Nordic Noir crime fiction:

Utopian and dystopian images of the Nordic countries existed long before what we now call Nordic noir. Perhaps BBC4 has just been very successful in starting the current trend. I think many people like me liked The Killing and The Bridge because of the brilliant characters. Actually, I don't have a TV here in Denmark.

Has there been a growth of interest in the Nordic Model lately?

It goes in waves. There has been a renaissance since the 2008 crash. When I started teaching a course on the Nordic model at UCL in 2000 I wondered how long it would be relevant and whether a course on the Baltic region would make more sense. But there's a renewed interest – the question is where does it go?'

What does she most like about Denmark?

Cycling. Denmark lives up to its reputation for being cycle-friendly and I don't have a car here – we've bought a tandem.

Something tells me Mary is staying.

WHEN WE TALK about *Norden*, or the Nordic region, we are
dealing with five nation states who have five – at least five
– different ways of thinking about their own national
narratives, five different ideas about European integration,
and five different ways of imagining what Europe as a
political entity actually means. It is also interesting to
explore how the intertwined history of Nordic relations
with Europe has impacted on levels of cooperation between
the Nordic states themselves, because the two are often
closely related.

A look at the map of the region shows us five sovereign
nation states – Finland, Denmark, Iceland, Norway and
Sweden – and three autonomous territories – the Faroe
Islands, Greenland and Åland. We often think about these
five states as small countries, or at least there is a self
perception that they are small countries. Actually, in the
context of the European Union, the Nordic countries are
neither among the largest states in terms of population, but
nor are they – with the exception of Iceland – among the
smallest. There are, when you think of it, quite a few EU
member states with populations around the five million
mark. With its population of 5.3m, Scotland may be only
half the size of Sweden, but it is very similar to Denmark,
Finland and Norway, with 5.7, 5.5 and 5.3m, respectively.

As to European integration, the Nordic countries have
distinctly diverse experiences. Denmark joined the European
Communities as part of the first enlargement in 1973,
together with the UK and Ireland. There had been earlier
negotiations during the 1960s, but membership was vetoed
by the French President Charles de Gaulle. Eventually,
Danish membership was confirmed by a majority of 63.3 per
cent in a referendum in October 1972.

Since then, though, Denmark has acquired a reputation
for Euro-scepticism, or at least for a commitment to a looser

intergovernmental union than the more politically ambitious idea of a supranational union.

Thorsten Borring Olesen, a historian at Aarhus University, has described Denmark as one of the pioneers of finding ways to limit Europeanisation, above all through a constitutional clause that can be used to trigger referenda when new policies imply any transfer of sovereignty.[1] That has meant that Denmark has had eight referenda since 1972. After Ireland, no EU state has had more referenda than Denmark, and those on the Maastricht Treaty in 1992, and on the Euro in 2000 produced 'no' votes.

In response to the 'no' to the 1992 Maastricht Treaty, which formally created the European Union and laid down some far-reaching ambitions for political union, the Danish Government negotiated opt-outs in four different areas in an agreement signed at the EU summit in Edinburgh in December 1992. These opt outs were on economic and monetary union, common foreign and security policy, justice and home affairs and European citizenship. In a second referendum on Maastricht in 1993, a majority voted for the Treaty, including the negotiated opt-outs.

After the general election in 2015, it looked as if Eurosceptic forces might become more prominent again because the government, led by the centre-right Venstre party, had to rely on the parliamentary support of the Eurosceptic Danish People's Party. But in the autumn of 2016, this party became embroiled in a scandal over the misuse of European funds for political purposes, and it was not clear if this would affect their electoral support.

The most recent Danish referendum on European

---

1 Thorsten Borring Olesen, 'Denmark in Europe 1973–2015: Processes of Europeanization and 'Denmarkization'', *Journal of Contemporary European Research*, 11, 4 (2015), pp. 312–329.

matters in December 2015 also produced a majority for 'no'. Although ostensibly it was about the highly technical matter of opting in to European cooperation on justice and policing, it was inevitably seen as a testing of the water on what people thought more generally.

The Danish *Rigsfællesskab*, or commonwealth, also includes the Faroe Islands and Greenland, which have had home rule since 1948 and 1979 respectively. When Denmark joined the European Economic Community in 1973, the Faroe Islands remained outside the EEC. Greenland followed Denmark into the EEC in 1973, but left in 1985.

Norway, like Denmark, took part in the EU enlargement negotiations in the 1960s and 1970s but its electorate rejected membership in an advisory referendum in September 1972. 53.5 per cent voted against joining the EC. The same thing happened in 1994, and the difference between Yes and No did not actually shift all that much in those intervening decades.

Norway is often cited as an example of a state which is a member of the single market, the EEA and of Schengen, without being a full member of the EU. The historian Francis Sejersted, for example, noted that Norway had implemented the vast majority of EU directives. Referring to a source from 2004, he wrote: 'Through its membership in the EEA Norway has followed through on 1,486 of the 1,494 EU directives, which is more than Sweden, an EU member, has managed.'[2]

Sweden and Finland have slightly different stories. During the Cold War, both were prevented from joining the European Community by their neutrality. In Finland especially, membership of western organisations was unthinkable because the cornerstone of Finnish foreign

---

2 Sejersted, Francis. *The Age of Social Democracy: Sweden and Norway in the Twentieth Century*, Princeton: Princeton University Press, 2011, p.482.

policy was the 1948 Treaty of Friendship, Co-operation and Mutual Assistance with the USSR, signed after Finland's defeat by the USSR in 1944. Finland was never part of the Eastern Bloc, but that security relationship and Finland's neutrality were a crucial part of relations with other organisations. Sweden also remained non-aligned throughout the Cold War period and joined neither the European communities nor NATO.

For both Sweden and Finland, therefore, applications for membership of the European Union came in the context of a major reconfiguration of security policy after the end of the Cold War. Both states joined in 1995, along with another formerly neutral state, Austria. Finland is the only Nordic country to date that has joined the Euro. In Denmark and Sweden it was rejected in referenda in 2000 and in 2003 respectively.

Finally, there is Iceland. It also remains outside the European Union. Like Norway, it is a member of the EEA. The question of EU accession was debated seriously for the first time after the 2008 financial crash. The new government elected in 2009 applied for membership, backed by a Parliamentary vote. But in 2015 it was announced that the application was being withdrawn.

So, there are five very different stories of the Nordics and the EU, and this is also the story of five different referenda on Europe in the Nordic countries between 1992 and 1994, with very different outcomes. Can we really talk about a common Nordic approach to Europe?

There did seem to be more enthusiasm in Finland than in Sweden for joining, at least during the early 1990s, although the turnout in the Swedish referendum was higher than that in Finland. Writing in 1992, the historian Henrik Meinander suggested that Finland's enthusiasm for EU membership is explained by the traumatic experiences of Finnish history, especially the period 1939–44 when Finland fought – and was defeated by – the Soviet Union, with significant territorial losses. The Finnish referendum to join the EU came at a time of considerable turbulence: a very serious economic crisis within Finland, and political disorder in the former Soviet Union. Meinander writes that 'membership of the EU has been felt to be not only a significant improvement in national security but also a kind of emotional homecoming,' a sense of being liberated from that difficult security relationship with Russia and becoming part of Europe.[3] And as the IT sector boomed in the late 1990s, the Finnish government used its new position within the EU to launch the so-called Northern Dimension, which still exists as a cooperation policy between the EU, Russia, Norway and Iceland.

As in any referendum, behind the neat percentages lie some very complex coalitions of different political, social and economic interests. In brief, among the main supporters of EU membership were the big industrial and employers' federations and often the leadership of the big political parties of both left and right of centre, although the Social Democrats in particular are often split on the question. Often, there seems to be a split between the cosmopolitan elites in metropolitan areas and those living and working in the more peripheral and rural districts – a bit like Brexit perhaps. But, unlike Brexit, a lot of Eurosceptics in the Nordic nations, the 'no' voters, have come from the political left, from those worried about protecting the welfare state and the public sector.

The referenda campaigns all focused on national sovereignty – they were all overlaid by questions about

3   Henrik Meinander, 'On the brink or in between? The conception of Europe in Finnish identity', in Mikael af Malmborg and Bo Stråth, eds, *The Meaning of Europe* (Oxford: Berg, 2002), pp. 149–168, 166.

Danish-ness or Finnish-ness or Norwegian-ness in relation to the EU. But there was also a broader question of Nordic identity in all these debates about EU membership.

We need to understand *Norden* as a historical region that is not fixed or bounded. It is also an unstable concept, the meaning of which has fluctuated over time. *Norden*, literally 'the North', is but one way of imagining this north-eastern part of Europe. How we think of it might also depend on our vantage point. Thus, what is understood in Scotland as 'Nordic' and how the term is used, might be very different to how Nordic is understood in Denmark, Finland, or Greenland, say.

Norden (or Scandinavia) cannot be seen in isolation, it must also be seen in the broader international context, and especially in relation to Europe. The way in which this is done has parallels to British thinking about Europe: one travels 'to' or even 'down to' Europe, from the Scandinavian north. In other words, although the Nordic region is indisputably part of Europe *Norden* has often been imagined, or self-imagined, as a relatively peripheral part of the continent. On the other hand, *Norden* has also been seen as an alternative to Europe. We can make a strong case that Nordic cooperation and integration has developed in tandem with the ebbs and flows of European integration.

It should be noted that regional cooperation was largely limited, at least during the Cold War period, to the so-called soft areas of policy – welfare, law, culture and the arts. But among its most enduring and lasting achievements was the establishment of the Nordic Passport Union in 1957, nearly 40 years before Schengen was implemented. This has actually been challenged in recent years, with new border controls emerging during the European refugee crisis. More ambitious schemes for Nordic cooperation, such as proposals for a Scandinavian defence union in the late

1940s, and for a Nordic customs union in the late 1960s, failed to produce agreement.

But, despite important differences in domestic and foreign policies within the Nordic countries, there was a certain amount of coherence in the Nordic region during the Cold War period. The region was also seen as remarkably peaceful. The Danish and Norwegian applications to join the European Communities during the 1960s did not really threaten to disrupt this balance either, because for neutral Finland and Sweden, as already noted, membership remained a political impossibility, at least for the time being.

On the other hand, when European integration entered a more dynamic phase in the 1990s, Nordic cooperation and the idea of a coherent Nordic region was questioned. Schengen, the Single Market, the Maastricht Treaty and the very dramatic events of 1989/91 – the fall of communism, the reunification of Germany and the collapse of the USSR – all presented a profound challenge to ways of thinking about the Nordic region: geopolitically, in terms of its position between East and West and ideologically, in terms of a Nordic model as a social democratic middle way between the extremes of communism and capitalism. It would not be too much of an exaggeration to view that period as a kind of Nordic identity crisis, especially in Sweden. It was a period when many taken-for-granted aspects of 20th-century history in the Nordic nations were up for question.

That change in the international security situation also coincided with a severe economic crisis in Finland and Sweden, and a breakdown in political consensus that was felt especially in Sweden which, since 1932, had been largely dominated by social democratic governments. The Swedish decision to apply for EU membership was announced by the Social Democratic prime minister Ingvar Carlsson in 1990, and came as something of a shock.

Carlsson's successor, the Conservative Carl Bildt, who was in office between 1991 and 1994, enthusiastically embraced the idea of Europe. In doing so, moreover, he also explicitly rejected the idea of the Nordic model as 'outdated'. The future seemed to lie not in Norden, but in Europe. With the old neutrality constraints now removed by the physical removal of the Berlin Wall and the Iron Curtain, and the demise of the Soviet Union, EU applications could be prepared in both Sweden and Finland and were submitted in 1991 and 1992 respectively. Norway also submitted a new application for membership.

For the Nordic region there were several possible responses to all these changes. Firstly, there was the possibility that the Nordic countries could function as a bloc within the European Union. Not surprisingly, the European question dominated debates in the Nordic Council during the early 1990s, with some arguing for a strengthened Nordic Council as a platform for a co-ordinated Nordic bloc within Europe, coupled with the ambition to influence European policy making, and especially European social policy, in a Nordic way.

But each different government pursued its own negotiations, and it became rather difficult to realise a common Nordic strategy. In a contribution to a recent book on Nordic cooperation, Thorsten Borring Olesen and Johan Strang suggest that EU membership by some Nordic nations meant the official institutions of Nordic cooperation (the Nordic Council) were weakened but that there was also an increase in the possibilities for informal cooperation between Nordic ministers, heads of government and civil servants.[4] But that was increasingly taking place in Brussels.

4   Thorsten Borring Olesen and Johan Strang, 'European challenge to Nordic institutional cooperation: Past, present and future', in Johan Strang, *Nordic Cooperation: A European region in transition*, London: Routledge, 2016, pp. 27–47.

Secondly, events during the 1990s also saw the emergence of alternative ways of thinking about northern Europe. The end of the Iron Curtain and the reunification of Germany gave impetus to the idea of a Baltic Sea region. The expectation was that the newly independent Baltic states – Lithuania, Latvia and Estonia – would soon become candidates for EU membership. They did join in 2004. The early 1990s was a period of rediscovery, a re-opening of contacts between the northern Nordic nations and the southern shores of the Baltic Sea.

But, at the same time, the idea of a Nordic region did not disappear. The early 1990s saw some profound rethinking about the historical meanings of *Norden* and its relation to Europe. Some academics – particularly in an influential anthology on the cultural construction of *Norden* published in 1997 – argued for a Nordic distinctiveness in terms of its deep historical roots: a Lutheran, social democratic, consensual *Norden*, in contrast to a Europe that was dominated by Christian Democracy, Catholicism and capitalism.[5]

What few could have foreseen in the 1990s was the remarkable renaissance of the idea of a distinctive Nordic region, and in particular the idea of a Nordic model. Since the 2008 financial crisis, the Nordic model has made a definite comeback. *The Economist*, in 2013, produced a special report on the Nordics as the next supermodel,[6] and a great deal of attention has been given recently to the Nordic countries in international rankings on happiness, openness, gender equality, education and the like. This has coincided

---

5   Øystein Sørensen and Bo Stråth, eds, *The Cultural Construction of Norden*, Oslo: Scandinavian University Press, 1997.

6   'The Nordic countries: The next supermodel' (Leader), *The Economist*, 2 February 2013.

with a tremendous interest in aspects of Nordic culture: crime dramas, design, food, knitwear, lifestyle. The latest obsession in the UK seems to be *hygge*.

The Nordic countries also attracted attention in the American presidential debate, at least in its primary stages. And in May 2016, President Obama invited the five Nordic prime ministers to a summit meeting in the White House and said very nice things about them, which were much reported. So, indisputably, the idea of a Nordic model has regained visibility, especially since 2008, but at the same time there is very little agreement about what it means.

Once upon a time, the Nordic model was identified as a social democratic model, so much so that the Swedish Social Democratic Party applied in 2011 to the Swedish patent office to have copyright of the term. They had invented it, they reckoned. The application was upheld, but the ruling has since been challenged by the Nordic Council, among others, which argues the Nordic model is 'part of the political heritage of the whole Nordic region and its people,' and cannot be associated with just one political party in one country.

Even in Sweden, it would be fair to say, there are now very different political visions of what the Nordic model might be. On the one hand, there has been a concern to try and overhaul the traditional social democratic model and redefine it for future generations, as in the 2014 *Sørmarka Declaration* which came from the Nordic Social Democratic Cooperation Committee (SAMAK) and was supported by a report from the research foundation Fafo.[7] But, on the other hand, there have also been attempts to redefine the Nordic model on the centre right, led by the Swedish conservatives

---

7 Sørmarka Declaration 'We Build the Nordics' available at www.samak. info/wp-content/uploads/2015/11/Sormarka-declaration_English.pdf.

2

who were in office between 2006 and 2014, and presented in a pamphlet distributed at the World Economic Forum in Davos in 2011.[8]

These statements (the Davos pamphlet and the Sørmarka declaration) have much in common: the commitment to the welfare state, the emphasis on the importance of work, references to innovation, openness, gender equality and environmental sustainability. What seems to differ is the interpretation of how the Nordic nations got there. Is the Nordic model the legacy of years of social democratic government or the product of a much more deeply embedded historical distinctiveness? Is it, as *The Economist* tried to suggest in 2013, a kind of new middle way between the old ideological polarities, harking back to the 1930s? Or is it no longer a general social model, but one that is much more specific, so that we can talk about a Nordic model of gender equality, or of life-long learning, or of elderly care, etc? What it really seems to suggest is that we have to talk about Nordic *models*, rather than a singular Nordic model.

The renaissance of the idea of the Nordic model has been accompanied by new initiatives in Nordic cooperation, significantly in areas that were not previously featured prominently, such as defence. In 2010, the Swedish historian Gunnar Wetterberg made a provocative proposal to revive the idea of a Nordic federation which, he argued, would give the Nordic countries a seat at the G20 meetings – among other things.

But there are clearly limits to Nordic cooperation and regional identity. National identities within the Nordic

---

8   A forthcoming PhD thesis from UCL by Tom Hoctor examines the implications of this for Westminster political debates. The Davos pamphlet 'The Nordic Way' is available at www.globalutmaning.se/wp-content/uploads/sites/8/2011/01/Davos-The-nordic-way- final.pdf

region are expressed in terms of differences between neighbours. Think of the Danish stereotype of the uptight politically correct Swede (so compellingly explored in the Danish-Swedish hit series *The Bridge*) or the Swedish stereotype of the silent Finn. The rivalries when Sweden and Denmark play each other at football, or when Finland play Sweden at ice hockey, are every bit as strong as when England play Scotland at football or rugby.

Yet, unlike European integration, Nordic cooperation and the Nordic regional identity have never been controversial. There may have been indifference, especially towards the official institutions of Nordic cooperation. There is the old chestnut of the mutual comprehensibility – or not – of the Scandinavian languages. But most Nordic citizens will probably acknowledge Nordic-ness as a layer of their identity, and very few will show open hostility towards the idea. It is impossible to talk about a Nordic-scepticism in political and popular opinion in the same way we can talk about Euroscepticism. And while national identity can be defined against Europe, Nordic and national identities do not tend to compete, they mutually reinforce each other.

We do tend to talk about all of this in terms of nation states: 'Denmark wants', 'Britain thinks', 'Britain rejects', or whatever. And this makes some sense, because we put the European negotiations into the hands of national governments and officials. But nation states are of course an amalgamation of many different regionalisms and localisms. One of the main issues in Danish politics at the moment is the growing divide between core and periphery, between the big cities like Copenhagen and Aarhus, and so-called *udkantsdanmark*, the peripheral areas of the west and south. It is a divide expressed in terms of economic and social inequality, but also in terms of political and cultural differences, which are remarkably strong in what is really quite a small and geographically compact country. And, of course, these also affect attitudes to Europe.

This reminds us that there is not just a history to all this, but also a geography. Loyalties to Europe or to Nordic cooperation are shaped by your vantage point. The Nordic Passport and Social Security unions had quite concrete impacts. Above all, they enabled tens of thousands of Finnish citizens to seek work in Sweden in the 1960s, and today, if you visit a bar in Copenhagen or Oslo, you are as likely to find the staff working there talking Swedish as Danish or Norwegian. The best-known example of cross border cooperation is of course the Øresund region between Copenhagen and Malmö, which has emerged in particular following the opening of the bridge across the Øresund in 2000 – yes *that* bridge.

But at the beginning of January in 2016, Sweden announced it was introducing – reintroducing – border controls. If you take the train now from Copenhagen to Malmö, you have to show your papers. That is a challenge not just for Schengen, but for half a century of Nordic Passport Union. Even two short years ago both challenges would have seemed unthinkable to most people, as indeed were the Brexit vote and Trump's election.

In conclusion, the story of *Norden* and the EU is above all one of complexity. There is no single Nordic model of European integration. It is a story of contingency and constantly shifting ideas, ideologies and identities. It is not static but constantly changing.

3

Lessons from Iceland

JÓN BALDVIN HANNIBALSSON

ICELAND

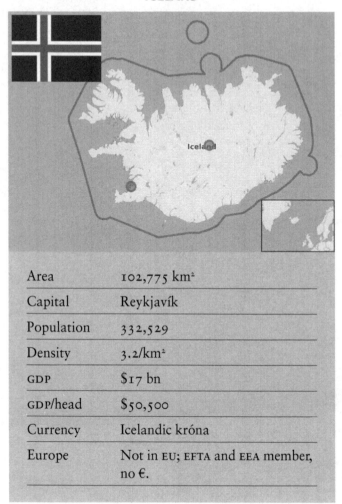

Area	102,775 km^2
Capital	Reykjavík
Population	332,529
Density	3.2/km^2
GDP	$17 bn
GDP/head	$50,500
Currency	Icelandic króna
Europe	Not in EU; EFTA and EEA member, no €.

JÓN BALDVIN HANNIBALSSON is an Icelandic politician and diplomat who led the Social Democratic Party (SPD) and was responsible for Iceland's entry to the EEA in the 1990s.

That's an accurate but wholly inadequate description of the 70-something who bounded into Scotland to speak at Nordic Horizons' Brexit conference, wowed the audience, met Nicola Sturgeon and Mike Russell along with Faroese MP Bjørt Samuelsen and then bounced onto STV's *Scotland Tonight* the same evening before flying back to Iceland with his wife Bryndís Schram, an actress, linguist, writer and TV personality.

His short but pithy TV contribution was still doing the rounds on YouTube as Jón Baldvin touched down at Keflavik.

Provocative, funny and thoughtful – the North Atlantic

pairing of Jón Baldvin and Bjørt Samuelsen seems to have prompted a subtle change of policy direction from the Scottish Government. Days later it announced the option of joining the EEA in any post-independence scenario would be added to their policy option list. Not bad for a long weekend in Edinburgh. But then Jón Baldvin is used to making an impact.

Like most Icelanders (with a part Norwegian/ part Celt DNA) Jón Baldvin has lived at full throttle in a great many places. He began his higher education in Scotland rather than his beloved Iceland, with an MA in Economics from Edinburgh University in 1963. Why did he choose Edinburgh?

> A close friend, Dr Hermann Pálsson, a prominent Icelandic scholar of Gaelic languages and culture and a professor at Edinburgh University, advised me to do so. But there was another and a more practical reason. The tuition fee at the time was less than 20 pounds sterling. Although I spent my summers as a deck-hand on board Icelandic deep-sea trawlers, earning a lot of money, the generosity of Scottish taxpayers helped me make the right decision.

Jón Baldvin then moved to Sweden and studied labour-market economics in the context of the Nordic model at Stockholm University, before returning home to do teacher training at the University of Iceland in 1965. 'It was never a question of not returning home. We were four brothers. All studied abroad, all returned home.'

For many Scots, life as a teacher means the end of having controversial views – in public at least. Not Jón Baldvin. From 1964 until it closed three years later, Jón Baldvin was editor of *Frjáls þjóð* (the Free Nation newspaper). Under his direction the paper even-handedly opposed the presence of American bases on Icelandic soil during peacetime and the United People's Socialist Party for their meek subservience to the Soviet Union.

Jón Baldvin continued as a teacher and journalist until 1970 when he became founder and rector of Ísafjörður College, in his hometown, the only FE college in the remote Westfjords region (1970–79), managing to fit in a year at Harvard before becoming editor of the Social Democratic Party-supporting newspaper *Alþýðublaðið* for three years (1979–1982).

He was a member of Parliament (Althingi – 1982–98), leader of the Social-Democratic Party (1984–96) and Minister of Finance (1987–1988) before settling into the job he most relished – Icelandic Minister of Foreign Affairs and External Trade (1988–1995). That was when family connections became particularly useful:

> My eldest brother was the first one from Western Europe to graduate from Moscow University after the war. His expertise in Soviet affairs and contacts with dissidents came in handy, when I got involved as foreign minister of a NATO-country, in support of the Baltic countries' independence struggle.

That momentous foreign policy move by tiny Iceland occurred in 1991 when Jón Baldvin recognised the independence of Lithuania – the only western foreign minister to arrive on the scene when Soviet troops tried to suppress the secession bid by attacking the TV station, killing 14 Lithuanian civilians and wounding 600 others. Jón Baldvin quickly began the process of establishing diplomatic connections between Lithuania and Iceland, and the Baltic state became a member of the United Nations six months later and a member of the EU in 2004. Today, in the grounds of the Lithuanian Parliament, one of the remaining barricades from January 1991 bears the inscription 'To Iceland – they dared when others remained silent'. For his personal role in recognising Lithuanian independence, Jón Baldvin was awarded the Commander's Grand Cross of the Order of the Lithuanian Grand Duke and made an honorary citizen of Vilnius – and, more recently, an honorary doctor of Vilnius University.

3

A few months after his bold trip to Lithuania, Jón Baldvin made Iceland the first nation to recognise the independence of Estonia and Latvia. He was later given the Estonian Order of the Cross of Terra Mariana, 1st Class, and today, a plaque commemorating Iceland's support sits on the wall of the Foreign Ministry in Tallinn. Its address makes an even greater statement of Estonia's enduring gratitude – *Islandi väljak* – 'Iceland Square'. His important role in firming up the teetering steps of the new Republic of Latvia was recognised with the Order of the Three Stars (3rd class). Recently, Iceland's role in support of the Baltic nations' struggle for restored independence has been made the subject of a documentary film, *Those Who Dare*. This was a joint project of Icelandic and Baltic film producers. It has been shown on TV in many countries, especially in the Baltic and East European region. Perhaps it would be of interest for a Scottish audience?

In December 1991, Jón Baldvin once again became the first foreign minister in the world to recognise a new sovereign nation as Croatia declared independence. Had he become a sort of patron saint of small nations struggling to escape from imperial control? Why?

> Well, I had become convinced that the breakup of the federation of Yugoslavia was inevitable and that the international community should recognise that fact and, accordingly, assist in the establishment of the constituent republics, in an orderly manner – to avoid the outbreak of a bloody civil war. But, as usual, the major powers had different agendas. Subsequently they failed to prevent a cruel civil war in Europe's backyard.

Later, Jón Baldvin served as Iceland's Ambassador to the United States and Mexico (1998 to 2002), in Finland, Estonia, Latvia and Lithuania (2002 to 2005) and as ambassador to Ukraine from 2004 to 2006.

But was it wise for the Foreign Minister of such a small country to run the risk of conflict with the Soviet Union by openly supporting Baltic freedom? In a recent interview Jón Baldvin said:

> The leaders of the West at the time were not following up on their rhetoric about democracy and national self-determination. Why not? Because they had, unwisely, placed all their bets for ending the Cold War on the political fate of President Gorbachev. Nothing should be said or done which undermined his position. If he were to be deposed, the hard-liners would come back. And there was a lot at stake. We might return to the Cold War – and even risk armed conflict in Eastern Europe.
>
> That's why President Bush (Sr) made his notorious 'chicken speech' in Kiev in late 1991, appealing to the Ukrainians 'not to succumb to extreme nationalism,' but to remain loyal to the Soviet Union in the name of peace and stability. This speech by an American president would have been music to the ears of (Vladimir) Putin, who has long mourned the demise of the Soviet Union as 'the greatest geo-strategic disaster of the twentieth century.'
>
> This was why (German) Chancellor Kohl and (French) President Mitterrand jointly wrote a letter to (Lithuanian) President Landsbergis, appealing to him to postpone their declaration of independence and instead negotiate with the Soviets without preconditions. This is why US high officials gave the same message to the Baltic freedom fighters in Vilnius, Riga and Tallinn.
>
> And this is why, since the voices of the leaders of the Baltic independence movements were not listened to, I tried to lend my voice to theirs in Western forums – especially NATO. This is why I responded, alone among NATO foreign ministers, to Baltic leaders' appeal to come and stay with them in January 1991, when the Soviets had decided to use force to crack down on their independence movements and to bring about regime change.
>
> This is why, when the hard-liners' attempted coup d'état in Moscow August 1991 had failed, I decided to use that window of opportunity – the power vacuum and confusion in Moscow at that

time – to invite the foreign ministers of all three Baltic states to Reykjavik to formalise the recognition of their restored independence. By doing so, I hoped to start a process that would become irreversible. That turned out to be right. To my mind, this is an example of 'the solidarity of small nations' which, under the correct circumstances, can succeed when the leaders of major powers fail.[1]

All of this took place before Jón Baldvin took the step that brought him to the attention of Scotland in 2016, master-minding Iceland's entry to the EEA in 1994 as Chief negotiator on the European Economic Area Agreement 1989–93.

Here Jón Baldvin reflects on Iceland's decision to join EFTA in the 1970s and the EEA two decades later and explains how Iceland achieved exemptions on fishing and agriculture – the pros and cons of that – and the temporary post-crash desire to be in the Euro. By the way, Jón Baldvin welcomes the idea of an independent Scotland joining the EEA. The question is: will Scotland manage to get a deal in EU negotiations, including exemptions from the common fisheries and agricultural policies, as Iceland managed to do in the early '90s, with strong support from their EFTA partners?

Jón Baldvin's answer – 'You can only find out at the negotiating table.'

---

1   Kourosh Ziabari, *Fair Observer* 2015 <www.fairobserver.com/region/europe/iceland-will-not-join-the-european-union-54680/>.

1   From Rags to Riches

Icelanders began the 20th century as the poorest of the poor in Europe. During the course of the century, we went from rags to riches. Around the end of the century, Icelanders had become the third richest country in Europe – in terms of income per capita – only surpassed by Luxembourg and Norway. Three small countries, by the way. Perhaps already a lesson to be learned.

Three major factors explain this success story: (1) home rule, (2) access to foreign capital, (3) tariff-free access to foreign markets. We could add a high level of education, speeding up technological transfer. Icelanders were never so poor that they were illiterate.

Iceland's independence struggle from Denmark underwent three major phases: home rule in 1904; a fully sovereign state 1918 (but in royal union with Denmark); severing the royal union with Denmark in 1944 by establishing the Republic of Iceland.

Regaining legislative and executive powers from faraway Copenhagen to Reykjavík was a turning point. Independence turned out to be a pre-condition for economic success. Another lesson to be learned?

2   Economic Model

The economic model also had three major dimensions: first, the ease with which technological transfer was accomplished; the acquisition of skills that enabled us to build a major fishing fleet and to start doing for ourselves what foreigners had been doing in Icelandic waters for centuries – and doing it better. Second, access to foreign capital, mainly Danish/ Scandinavian and third, free access to foreign markets for our fish products, in the British Isles, but also in Mediterranean Europe (Spain, Portugal, Italy and Greece) for salted fish (*baccalau islandiae*).

Summing up: Political independence was the driving force. Access to technology, foreign capital and markets – favourable external factors – were a precondition. But with the outbreak of World War l this liberal era came to an abrupt end. Protectionism became the order of the day, closing the window of opportunity for developing countries like Iceland. For an export-oriented developement economy, the closing of markets was a fatal blow. Iceland was hard hit by the Great Depression.

3   World War II

When Iceland became a sovereign state in 1918, it was written into the constitution that Iceland would be eternally neutral. The Second World War taught us better. Denmark and Norway were occupied by Nazi-Germany. Hitler had plans to occupy Iceland as well, but the British managed to pre-empt them. When the Icelandic prime minister was woken up during the night of occupation, he only asked one question: 'Which ones are they – the British or the Germans?' When the police told him they were apparently British, he simply said: 'OK, thank God, then I can go back to sleep.'

The British soon had other preoccupations though, and left it to the Americans to take over. This was done by bilateral agreement. Thus started a long-term Icelandic/American relationship in defence and security.

Iceland's military significance turned out to be crucial during the battle of the Atlantic, against German submarine warfare. In the words of a later secretary general of NATO, Iceland was the substitute for an unsinkable air-carrier for the allies. Had the battle of the Atlantic not been won, the 'arsenal of democracy' – the US – would not have been able to supply the arms for the Red Army on the Eastern front, and the invasion of Normandy would hardly have been accomplished.

Thus our naive dreams about eternal neutrality were brutally shattered. Iceland became a founder member of NATO in 1948. In 1951 – during the Korean War – we signed a bilateral defence agreement with the Americans. Until 2006 American forces were stationed in Iceland as a naval and air base on behalf of NATO.

While Europe was tearing itself to pieces and European cities were being bombed into ruins, Icelanders made a lot of money trying to feed the British. Although not a belligerent, we lost more people at sea during the war – in proportion to our population – than many of the belligerents themselves. At the end of it all, while Europe lay in ruins, Iceland had become rich. The Second World War was a turning point in our economic development.

4   The Cold War

The Cold War meant that Iceland continued to be in a pivotal position. Although we had not been combatants in the war, in a formal sense, the conflict had proven Iceland's military significance in the North Atlantic. This explains why Iceland, which had benefitted economically from the war, was nonetheless a recipient of the Marshall Plan for post-war reconstruction. This was highly significant in building up the infrastructure of the country.

5   The Cod Wars

Icelanders live by the sea, just like our cousins in the Faroe Islands and in Norway, before the Norwegians became filthy rich from their oil and gas. In order to protect our marine resources from over-exploitation, we became partners in an informal alliance of coastal states which fought for control over marine resources within expanded and exclusive economic zones (EEZ). Until then, the three-mile limit, imposed by British gunboat diplomacy, had been the more or

3

less accepted rule. When we started expanding our EEZ in stages from 1954 until we adopted the 200-mile limit in 1975, we landed in conflict with her Majesty's Royal Navy. Thus began the Cod Wars (1954–76).

Already in 1954 her Majesty's government placed an embargo on Iceland, closing the British market for our exports, which was meant to teach us a lesson. But this was during the Cold War. The Soviet Union offered to buy all the fish that Iceland could supply. So, the British forced Iceland into a long lasting trade relationship with the Soviet Union. We fed them our fish and they provided us with oil and Moskvitches – sturdy cars that could be used in the wilderness on Iceland's primitive roads.

In the autumn of 1958, the year I graduated from high school and started my studies at Edinburgh University, I had spent the summer as usual on a trawler in the North-Atlantic in the waters around Iceland, Greenland and Newfoundland. That was when the Icelandic government expanded our exclusive zone from four to 12 miles. The British sent in the Royal Navy. They repeated that in 1972 and 1975, when we expanded our EEZ to 50 and ultimately to 200 miles. We countered with guerrilla warfare on the high seas. Our small but manoeuvrable gunboats cut the gear from behind British trawlers, which had to be herded together under military protection.

The Royal Navy lost all three 'Cod Wars'. We won. We won partly because we had a better cause (protecting marine resources); partly because we were NATO-members, and could put pressure on the US superpower to restrain the enfeebled empire; and partly because we played the Cold War adversaries against each other. The Cod Wars also had a biblical undertone: David vs Goliath...

6   Nordic Co-operation

The five Nordics – Finland, Sweden, Norway, Denmark and Iceland (with a combined population of ca. 25 million) – have a long-established, close and structured cooperation network. There is also a West-Nordic union – Greenland, Iceland and the Faroe Islands – involving the North of Norway. Nordic cooperation is pursued at many levels: governments, parliaments, regions and municipalities. There are also people to people contacts at the level of students, teachers, trade unions, professional associations, scientific research and in the arts etc. Visa-free travel has for long been a fixture of Nordic cooperation. This meant, that when three of the Nordics had joined the EU, the rest of us had to join Schengen, to maintain our open borders. So we have maintained free movement of people amongst us, at the cost of giving up external border control.

Our first experience with European integration was within the framework of Nordic cooperation. This was long before EU-membership became an option. But for a small country like ours – with minimal bureaucracy – it has been very valuable. For instance, it saves us a lot of hard work, because we can copy the laws of fellow Nordic countries. We call it – in the name of efficiency – standardisation. Nordic cooperation is now – in the Post-Cold War era – being gradually extended to the newly independent Baltic countries (5+3). They are rapidly catching up – and 'we are stronger together'.

7   Iceland and the EU

Taking the next steps in European integration (EFTA and EEA) meant that Iceland had to implement radical, domestic reforms in the 1960s. As I mentioned we lost markets during the great depression because of protectionist policies everywhere. Our response was to build up a centralised, statist, protectionist economic system, which we maintained through the Second World War until the early 1960s.

It was almost a Soviet-type economy. The exchange-rate and currency transactions were state decreed; banks and investment funds were state run. Exports and imports were licensed and price controls widely applied. This was a system based on state sponsored favouritism – in essence, crony-capitalism *á la* Latin America. In order to fulfil the entrance requirements of a free-trade association like EFTA, we had to open up this semi-closed system. So, in the early 1960s, we initiated a series of reforms. We took significant steps towards an open market economy, at the initiative and under the leadership of my party, the Social Democrats. This often led to conflicts with entrenched special interests.

8   EFTA 1970

As a young economist – an Edinburgh-educated lad of not even 30 years – I found myself a member of the committee that was entrusted with negotiating our EFTA entry and preparing the Icelandic public for it. It was controversial, since it was instrumental in abolishing the established protectionist system. It caused temporary transitional hardship for domestic industrial production which had been built up behind tariff walls since the great depression.

In 1972 EFTA concluded a free trade agreement with the European economic community. This agreement covered industrial products but only limited tariff reductions for a restricted number of fish products. A step in the right direction, but far from satisfactory.

9   The EEA

The next major step was the EEA agreement (the European Economic Area). This comprehensive and dynamic (meaning continuously renovated) agreement was negotiated in

1989–93 but took effect 1994. The big question is: Why the EEA? Why didn't we simply join the European Union at the time?

The main explanation is that the EEA agreement is a product of the Cold-War era: before the fall of the Berlin Wall, before the liberation of Eastern Europe and before the unification of Germany, many of the EFTA countries were neutral. (Finland, Sweden, Switzerland and Austria). For political reasons they could not join a supra-national organisation, like the European Union. The EEA was conceived as an urgent interim solution, dictated by the political situation, but driven by economics.

Take into account that the seven EFTA countries were at that time more important as trading partners for the European Union than the United States and Japan put together. When small but strong countries gang up, they can make their weight be felt in the international arena. Sometimes the EEA is dubbed Jacques Delors' baby. Delors was the architect and the driving force behind both the internal market and the monetary union. The European Union under his leadership was totally preoccupied by those two enormous projects. Therefore, there was no time – nor resources – left to accept new members at the time. Nonetheless, for reasons of trade and economics, it was in the European Union's interest to conclude a free-trade agreement with their major trading partners, the EFTA countries. So, that's what we did. The EFTA countries (40+ millions) became partners in the internal market (300 millions). I sometimes designate us as being ¾ EU members.

All the EU–EEA countries operate under homogeneous rules and regulations, defining the four freedoms: free trade in goods, services, financial services and the free movement of people. Thus, the EEA countries enjoy the privileges and benefits of the largest free-trade area in the world (until

Brexit becomes effective some 500 million people), without being saddled by the less successful, common agricultural and fisheries policies or the ill-conceived and dysfunctional European Monetary Union (EMU).

10 A Fishy (Thorny) Issue

The declared policy of the EU – when it came to fish – was: no market access, without access to resources. This was totally unacceptable to a country like Iceland. Reciprocal access to markets, yes – but we had not fought three cod wars with Britain, only to open up our marine resources to the Spanish armada and the rest. That's why we said, right from the beginning, to our EFTA partners: You have to accept the principle of free trade in fish – just as for industrial products – within EFTA and make it a common EFTA negotiating position. Or else we can't go along.

After much soul searching and at the last moment, this was accepted. Why? Because fish was such a marginal thing for most of the other countries that they wouldn't let it thwart our solidarity. This generosity by our EFTA partners saved Iceland from being left alone in a hopeless negotiating position on our vital national interest. And, at the end of the day, it enabled us to turn the tables on the German dominated EU negotiating machine. We got free market access for our fish (which also benefited the Norwegians and the Faroese), without giving away any access to our resources. We also got an exemption from the right of establishment (investment) in our fishing sector, which holds still today. This is yet another lesson from the Icelandic experience. Would this precedent suffice to enable Scotland to get a similar deal on her own?

11 Political Controversy

Iceland is a (relatively) newly independent country. Icelandic politics are to this day very much moulded by the narrative of our independence struggle against Denmark. Political parties try to outdo each other in jealously guarding our national sovereignty against all-comers. That explains why the EEA agreement was hugely controversial. The fishing lobby was against it (fearing the loss of their monopoly of fishing rights in the Icelandic EEZ). The agricultural lobby was against it. Romantic nationalists, left and right, were against it.

Scare-mongering was stringent: German industrialists would buy our salmon rivers. The Spanish (fishing) armada would start fishing up to our shores. Portuguese immigrants would underbid our workers. At the last resort, our precious national language would be in danger of extinction. The conservatives (in opposition) were against it. The farmers' party and the reconstructed communist party – my partners in the government – ultimately turned against it. Even the feminists didn't see in it any liberating salvation.

The Icelandic parliament (Althingi) – the oldest in the world – spent more time debating the EEA than all the other EFTA parliaments combined. It took even more time in parliament than the adoption of Christianity 1,000 years ago!

So, how could we get it through? It was a lonely fight for me personally and my Social Democratic party. If put to a referendum, polls indicated that it would be rejected. So, after parliamentary elections in 1991 – which were fought mainly on the EEA issue – I proposed to the conservative opposition leader (Mr Oddsson) to make him prime minister, on condition his party changed tack and guaranteed a parliamentary majority for the EEA. He liked being PM, (but continued too long for his own good). So we rejected the proposal for a national referendum. In the end we scraped through in parliament. At long last it took effect on 1 January 1994.

When the EEA agreement was finally signed, it happened in Oporto in Portugal, which had the presidency of the EU at that time. I was then president of the EFTA ministerial council. The first one to sign was the Portuguese prime minister, (H) aníbal Cavaco Silva. Then I put my name to it: Hannibalsson. Then we stood up and shook hands and with a reference to our signatures I observed: 'This proves that Hannibal's influence has by now reached way beyond the Alps.'

12 The Economic Impact

In the period 1988–94, Iceland was suffering a serious economic recession. GDP-growth was negative year by year. The reasons were severely reduced catches and lower prices in foreign markets and deteriorating terms of trade. But the EEA agreement changed all that. When it started having an effect, our economy took off into a long-lasting boom. Exports increased at a pace. Foreign direct investment reached record levels. We enjoyed a healthy rate of growth year by year. The economy became increasingly diversified, through growing sectors of clean and renewable energy, information technology, pharmaceuticals etc.

Most economists agree that the EEA agreement was having a transformational effect, becoming a driving force of economic growth and general prosperity. Having been decried as endangering our national independence and accused of high treason for breaching the constitution – the EEA deal was now acclaimed as a masterpiece of negotiating skills. It was said to take care of our vital national interests, but deftly avoiding encroaching dangers that came with full membership. Those who had fought against it tooth and nail now used it as proof that we need go no further with European integration. The EEA agreement was said to be good enough. A good enough reason for EU-membership to be unnecessary.

13 What About National Sovereignty?

When the seven EFTA countries began negotiating the EEA in 1989, we construed a parallel administrative structure for 'decision-shaping and decision-making'. This meant that the EEA was a two pillar construction. Together the EFTA countries would, formally at least, have equal influence in the decision-making process. Also, there would have been a separate court to settle disputes.

But then the course of history caught up with us. The Berlin Wall came tumbling down; Eastern Europe was set free; the Soviet Union was no more. The Cold War was over. This meant that the neutrals among the EFTA countries felt free to cross the bridge and join the EU as full members in 1995. Also, the perennially democratic eccentrics in Switzerland rejected the EEA in a national referendum. What was left to shoulder the EFTA pillar was only Norway, Iceland and Lichtenstein – a little more than five million people, compared to 500 million on the other side.

This meant that the EFTA pillar could no longer be maintained on equal terms. Hence, the three of us on the EFTA side are in reality obliged to adopt the inner market legislation emanating from the Commission, without the institutional capacity to influence the legislation during the preparatory stage. Formally our parliaments can reject EU-proposals. In reality we never do, because as a consequence we would have to opt out from that part or function of the inner market. So, *de jure*, we maintain our legislative sovereignty; *de facto*, we adopt the inner market legislation.

In legal terms this means that we have transferred an important chunk of our legislative, executive and judicial sovereignty to the EU, without having any means of influencing the outcome. Is this acceptable? Well, *de facto* the three EFTA countries have accepted this situation for almost a quarter century. Earlier I told you the Icelandic administration found it very convenient to adopt or copy Nordic legislation. We call this process standardisation. We do this voluntarily and see nothing wrong with it.

To what extent has Scotland had to accept legislation from Westminster, without Scottish consent? To some, this voluntary transfer of sovereignty may be deemed unacceptable. To others – especially those in the orbit of small nations – this may be accepted as a practical necessity, a consequence of the irresistible force of globalisation which cannot be turned back.

14 The Crash

After almost a decade and a half of EEA driven economic growth – Icelanders suddenly found themselves in the abyss of national bankruptcy: the Crash of 2008. Although made in the USA, the contagious fever of financial disease spread around the globalised system. Eight years after the plague struck Europe, it is still in the grip of a deep recession.

But why Iceland? There are those who say that since the EEA agreement was given most of the credit for the boom, it should also accept the blame for the Crash. In other words: that it was all my fault. But our EFTA-partner, Norway, operates under the same rules and regulations of the inner market as Iceland does, yet there was no Crash there. So, we have to seek other explanations.

One of the best things we did in Iceland after the Crash was to set up an investigative commission – under the leadership of three wise men – to spell out the causes and consequences of the Crash. This they duly did in nine volumes and thousands of pages. Their conclusions are supported by massive evidence. Two right of centre governments, pursued a policy of turning Iceland into an international financial centre. It was all done under the guidance of neo-liberal ideology: markets are infallible, but government intervention is malevolent.

They began by privatising the fishing quotas. Instead of auctioning them off to the highest bidder – letting market forces prevail – they handed them out for free, despite the law stipulating our marine resources to be the common property of the nation. This act of political favouritism created a plutocratic elite *á la Rus*. Then they privatised the banks, ie they handed them out to business groups, favoured by the ruling parties. Again *á la Rus*. In almost no time at all, domestic commercial banks were turned into leveraged hedge funds, operating abroad, primarily in the city of London.

The danger signals had already started blinking by 2006. In early 2008, Willem Buiter, a world-renowned expert on financial crisis, delivered a confidential report on the Icelandic banking system. In this report he sounded the alarm: The business model of the Icelandic banks was utterly unsustainable. The accumulated foreign denominated debt – more than ten times Iceland's GDP – was way beyond the capacity of the Icelandic government, the Central Bank or even the taxpayer base to sustain. It was not a question of if – only when – it would burst. Then Mr Buiter proceeded to propose drastic emergency action for damage control. The official response was to lock up the report and do nothing.

After the Crash Iceland set a good example for others by setting up a special prosecutor's office to investigate financial crimes and bring those found guilty to justice. Many of the most prominent business leaders have been found guilty of various financial crimes, such as market manipulation, insider trading and a variety of fraudulent behaviour. This seems to confirm William Black's dictum: 'The best way to rob a bank is to own a bank.' The government, ministries and the Central Bank were all found wanting – not to speak of the media, mostly owned by the oligarchs. Later, when the names of two party leaders, three government ministers and up to 600 prominent business persons were found in the

Panama-papers, enlisting those trying to hide their wealth and financial income from the tax-authorities – Icelanders were not surprised.

15 Inside or Outside the EU/EMU?

I suppose the main question of interest to others, concerning this dismal drama, is the following: of those countries, hardest hit by the international financial crisis, which ones have done better, those inside the EU/EMU – or those outside? Iceland or Ireland? Iceland or Greece/Cyprus? In answering those questions we would do well by concentrating on the following: In which countries was unsustainable debt written off, which is the normal thing to do in bankruptcy courts? In which countries were taxpayers forced to bail out the banks to pay the debts of the oligarchs? And which countries could resort to the essential adjustment mechanism – when hard hit by external or domestic shocks – to regain competitiveness by growth-stimulating policies?

I am talking about the basic tools of nation-states for shock-absorption: the fiscal tools of adjusting the tax burden and public expenditures, eg by stimulus financing in a recession. And the monetary tools of adjusting the exchange rate and the rate of interest, to restore economic growth.

The facts speak for themselves: The countries hardest hit by the financial crisis inside the EU/EMU are still in the grip of a long-lasting recession. Few, if any, have regained lost GDP, counted in billions of euros and millions of lost jobs. Iceland has recovered much faster. There are four main reasons: devaluation has restored competitiveness and stimulated an export boom; there was no bail-out of the fallen banks; there was massive write-off of unsustainable debt; and external conditions turned out to be favourable. Loss of GDP through negative growth was therefore minimal and normal economic growth has been restored.

3

Since this book is about Scotland, I cannot resist mentioning the part played in this drama by a man named Gordon Brown, Scotland's prodigal son, I believe. When he, in his infinite wisdom, decided to include the Icelandic banks (which were mainly operating in the City of London), and the Central Bank – as well as the government of Iceland – on a list of terrorist organisations, alongside Al-Qaeda, he actually did us a favour – unknowingly, I presume. After that nobody in the whole of the universe would dare lend Iceland a penny. Even the IMF could no longer reasonably propose a bail-out of the banks. The whole of eternity would not have been sufficient for Iceland's 200,000 taxpayers to repay the banksters' debts.

So thanks in part to Gordon Brown there was no banking bail-out in Iceland. In spite of what I have said about Iceland's relatively speedy recovery, I do not want to leave you with the impression that all is well and dandy in my country; that the Crash has not left behind a legacy of economic pain and social disruption. It has. Two of our main banks were until recently owned by American hedge funds – a lethal cocktail, indeed. The explosion of debt through inflation has dispossessed many households. Many of the best and the brightest have emigrated to Norway or Canada. And the oligarchs, who escaped the Crash scot-free, by hiding their wealth offshore and in wealth-management funds in the City of London or Luxembourg, have been buying up companies and real estate at fire sale prices. Iceland is now a polarised society with a super-rich elite, a squeezed middle-class and increased poverty, where trust in our institutions has rapidly evaporated. After the Crash, the ideal Nordic welfare state has been severely weakened.

16 Are there any Lessons?

If there are any lessons worth learning by others, perhaps they are the following:

- **Independence.** National control of legislative, executive and judicial powers is essential as a driving force for economic progress.

- In an era of globalisation, nation states – especially small nations – must strike the **right balance** between national control and the transfer of sovereignty to international associations, in limited and clearly defined sectors.

- The **transfer of sovereignty**, in the name of homogeneity of the inner market of the EU, has not turned out to be problematic for the EFTA countries. It is an example of successful adjustment to the forces of globalisation.

- The EMU **is a failure.** It has deprived the weaker (deficit) member-states of the essential tools for adjusting to external shocks. Instead they are locked in a straight-jacket of **austerity**, which is the wrong recipe for dealing with recession. This lack of visionary leadership has left behind economic stagnation, social misery and deep political resentment. It is even endangering the cohesion of the European Union itself.

- If **Scotland,** after Brexit, wants to maintain the benefits of access to the inner market of the EU, without being burdened by the EMU or the ravages of the Common Fisheries Policy – the EEA **is tailor-made** for that purpose.

The question is: will Scotland now be able to make a deal with the EU as good as Iceland and Norway did, a quarter of a century ago? You can only find out the answer at the negotiating table.

4

A Reverse Greenland?

ULRIK PRAM GAD

GREENLAND

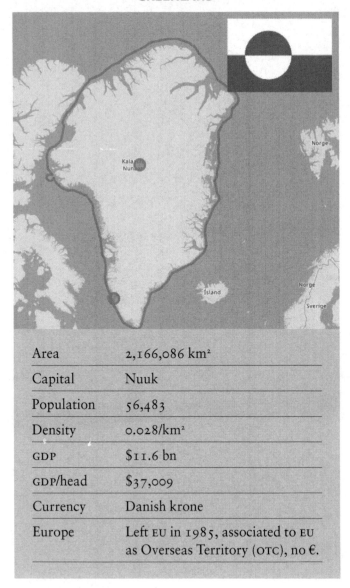

Area	2,166,086 km²
Capital	Nuuk
Population	56,483
Density	0.028/km²
GDP	$11.6 bn
GDP/head	$37,009
Currency	Danish krone
Europe	Left EU in 1985, associated to EU as Overseas Territory (OTC), no €.

ULRIK PRAM GAD was born and raised in Danish suburbs and provincial towns. He visited family friends in Sweden and has skied in Norway (cross-country, of course!) at least once a year since early childhood.

He consequently believes he speaks Norwegian and Swedish but occasionally lapses into some sort of Inter-Scandinavian mix.

Ulrik says he was raised as a standard Nordic left-wing Eurosceptic, but converted to Euro-Federalism as a reaction to the nationalism of the 1992 'No' campaign in the Danish referendum on the Maastricht Treaty:

> It dawned on me that in the face of problems like pollution and the adverse effects of globalisation, nation states are just powerless.

We need international cooperation. And we will not succeed if the most conservative member state can block everything – so we need cooperation to be supranational. And the only way to have that in a democratic way is to turn the whole thing into a federation. So my wife had to endure a fifty/fifty mix of Danish and European flags at our wedding.

All Ulrik's degrees come from the University of Copenhagen – but he has studied at six institutions in Denmark, Sweden, Norway… and Greenland.

As with most of our other speakers at the Nordic horizons conference, accidents, timely job offers and love seem to have guided Ulrik's career path:

After finishing my first undergraduate degree, I followed a friend looking for her Greenlandic family. But we couldn't afford the tickets so we had to apply for work. Fortunately, the man described as the right hand of the Greenlandic prime minister, top civil servant Kaj Kleist, decided he needed a right hand of his own.

So Ulrik worked in Nuuk for the Government of Greenland from 1998–2002 as a management assistant in the Cabinet Secretariat and as Head of the Department for Foreign Affairs. It was a bit ironic because Ulrik was a big convert to EU membership but two decades earlier, while Prime Minister Jonathan Motzfeldt and Kaj Kleist led the Greenlandic campaign to leave the EU.

Ulrik tried to finish a MA degree at the tiny University of Greenland, but could not combine it with a 70 hour working week and gave up. He says:

Always (in my self-understanding) I was the one who fought for oppressed minorities. So it was kind of a wake-up call to be in Nuuk; suddenly I was one of the 'evil colonial oppressors' even though I was working for the Greenlandic government. Consequently I decided to write my MA thesis on Greenlandic language policy and identity politics as a kind of self-therapy, when I got back to Denmark.

Ulrik then completed a PhD on the way Danish political debate casts Muslims as a threat, but was repeatedly distracted from that line of research by requests to write about Greenland. Including of course, Nordic Horizons' request to come and speak at our Brexit event in 2016.

Ulrik has recently taken up a position at the University of Aalborg to concentrate on postcolonial Arctic Politics and has just published a book on the triangular sovereignty game-playing between Greenland, Denmark and the EU.[1] He is currently writing on other aspects of Greenlandic nation building and foreign policy, like the effects of the US Thule Air Base on local hunters, and the very different choices taken by the Greenlanders and the Faroese when writing up their constitutions to separate from the Danish State.

1 Ulrik Pram Gad, *National Identity, Politics and Postcolonial Sovereignty Games: Greenland, Denmark, and the European Union*, Copenhagen: Museum Tusculanum Press, 2017.

GREENLAND IS OFTEN mentioned as one of the few territories that have left the EU, or the EEC as it was in 1985. Strange – people never seem to talk about Algeria, which also left back in 1962.

Anyway, during the Brexit campaign, most major news organisations in the UK sent a reporter to Nuuk, the capital of Greenland, only to report that Greenexit was a poor precedent for anything. Greenland's departure from the EEC does not fit the current EU membership dilemma facing Britain and Scotland in terms of the process, substance or size of the problem.

On the one hand, Greenland is a huge island, far up in the north. On the other hand, it has only 56,000 inhabitants – it is far from Europe and a very small community. But in one very specific way the case of Greenland is a precedent for the UK, because Brexit is not the first time the question of EU membership has acted as a catalyst for debates over devolution, constitutional reform and even independence.

If we go back to 1972, a huge majority in Greenland voted against EEC membership in the Danish referendum, but since Greenland was a constitutionally integrated part of Denmark, the island had to follow the Mother Ship into the EEC. This experience was pivotal in boosting the demand for Home Rule in Greenland. Particularly since the Faroe Islands were able to stay out of the EEC, due to their 1948 Home Rule arrangement. All of this created political pressure for a new Home Rule arrangement for Greenland which made it possible for the territory to withdraw from the EEC in 1985.

But, there is an even more important way in which the Kingdom of Denmark may serve as an instructive example for the UK, and that concerns the importance of constitutional pragmatism and the willingness on all sides to play games with sovereignty.

Of course the relevance of Denmark's experience only

really became clear after the British EU referendum, when it turned out that Scotland, Northern Ireland, London and Gibraltar had voted to remain, against the majority in England and Wales for leaving. These very diverse results opened up all kinds of questions about independence and sovereignty and devolution.

My contribution to this debate is informed by a book I have just finished writing on Greenland's experience leaving the EU. It was based on a project where a colleague and I were comparing Greenland's relationship to Europe with that of other small non-sovereign overseas territories like the British Virgin Islands and French Polynesia. However, the book was also based on four years I spent working in Nuuk, first as an assistant to the then Prime Minister, and then in the Department of Foreign Affairs.

I found that this idea of 'doing a reverse Greenland' was misrepresented in various ways when it was translated into the UK context, and that some of the arguments for dismissing it were therefore flawed. The basic message here is that the Danish case highlights how one sovereign state may comprise territories with a variety of formal and practical statuses vis à vis the European Union. Of course the UK, with all kinds of affiliated territories, entails some of the same diversity, but I think that the dynamics represented by Greenland and the Faroe Islands under Danish sovereignty might make some new opportunities visible that have not hitherto appeared in the British experience.

When Greenland left the EEC, there was no Article 50 in the European treaties. It would not have been relevant, anyway, because what took place was not the exit of a member state. Instead, part of a territory of a member state was exempted from membership. That, of course, was not a unilateral decision, it was formalised in a protocol to the treaties, signed by all member states. It was the result of tough negotiations; it did not just mean sending a letter.

Denmark remained a member state. The territory of Greenland was exempted from membership and transferred to a category of 'overseas countries and territories with constitutional links to a member state'. This category (OCT) already existed in the treaties, laying out a framework for how to associate post-colonial territories with the European communities; mainly devised in the beginning to facilitate the French empire, but most of the African countries it was meant for became independent before they ever entered this category.

As part of their negotiations, Greenland had to agree to special conditions. It was not a case of just adopting the OCT framework. Greenland had to agree to have a fisheries agreement, basically selling quotas and stocks for cash, to receive this preferential OCT status. At first, the negotiations between the EEC and Greenland were handled by Denmark, with mandates more or less rubber-stamped by the authorities in Nuuk, but increasingly over the years both the substantial preparation and the negotiations themselves were taken over by Nuuk and Greenlandic diplomats in Brussels.

The point here is that the EU process formed part of a general tendency towards devolution within the Kingdom of Denmark which also involved elements of foreign relations which had once been core to the sovereignty of the state. Actually, it could be argued that the Greenlandic Government started working in foreign affairs before anything was formally devolved within this area. You could even say that, in the beginning, they were doing stuff they had no permission for.

When the Arctic Council was formed in 1996, it was the Greenlandic Home Rule prime minister that was signing the founding documents – on behalf of Denmark, of course. But in 2005, Denmark informed diplomats in Copenhagen that Greenland and the Faroes could sign bilateral agreements with foreign states if they involved only devolved matters and provided that Denmark proper was not part of the *problematique*. In that sense, Greenland and the Faroe Islands are allowed to act on behalf of Danish sovereignty. And if we look beyond Denmark, it is not uncommon for states to mandate lawyers and private citizens, even NGO representatives and sometimes foreign nationals to represent them in international fora and negotiations. And if you go back in history, this was actually how diplomatic practice began, that a king asked someone somewhere to represent him and act on his behalf. What matters in diplomacy is that all parties acknowledge the credentials of the representative. In that sense, nobody doubted that Lars Emil Johansen from Greenland could sign for Denmark on the Arctic Council.

The zenith of this kind of thinking came in 2013 when Danish authorities agreed to launch an appeal at the WTO Board of Disputes, on behalf of the Faroe Islands, against the EU over a fisheries dispute. In a formal sense, Denmark was preparing to launch a case against itself, as an EU member state. Matters were eventually settled out of court before the case was launched. But the point remains that the Danes proved a state can actually be on both sides of the table at the same time, provided that everyone else around the table, and the folk back home, accept and trust that you can play multiple roles in a fair way.

Returning to the UK, and by no means trying to tell Scotland or Britain what to do, let me show you how it would look if 'Reverse Greenland' was used as a model. When she took over, Theresa May famously claimed that 'Brexit means Brexit', and everybody observed that did not really tell us anything. But, in the same speech, she also promised she was going to make a success of it.

If, as expected, Article 50 is activated on the basis of a Brexit majority in England and Wales, and if this involves the risk of Scottish secession and renewed troubles in Northern Ireland and isolation in Gibraltar, it could actually be quite difficult to describe the results of the Prime Minister's action as a success, particularly for the leader of a Conservative and Unionist party.

So the basic idea here is that, instead of triggering Article 50, or even if Article 50 is triggered, you could at some point backtrack within the two years of negotiations, backtrack from this insistence that the UK will leave as a single entity – the United Kingdom. You could backtrack and you could aim negotiations instead at a territorial exemption of England and Wales from UK membership. We could call it 'EngWexit' – though that is not a very graceful name. And the result would be that the United Kingdom, formally, would still be a member state. The UK would probably have to negotiate some sort of reduction of the voting rights to match the size of the population in Scotland and Northern Ireland (who would still be in the EU). And the crucial question of who would represent this member state, on what mandate and following what kind of procedures – that would all have to be solved within the UK. Presumably, ministers from Northern Ireland and Scotland would have to have central roles in making the decisions, and also going to Brussels and voting on things.

Maybe the main effect of formulating this perspective is to put the finger on, or turn the attention to, the fact that this might solve the problem for Northern Ireland, or Scotland, and perhaps Gibraltar, but of course it would leave *the* central problem on the table: what kind of relationship should England and Wales have with the EU and the single market? And it is the solution to this problem that would then determine future constitutional relationships inside the

4

United Kingdom. As the reporters on their trips to Nuuk found out, the inspiration for those relationships would have to be found elsewhere than in Greenland.

Now, I do not in any way claim that this is the most likely scenario. I do not even claim that it is, in the end, practically possible. It basically depends on what Brexit means, or rather: on what EngWexit means. And then it depends on whether politicians in London will allow their constitutional lawyers to be flexible and creative. But, when the chips come down, I do see a scenario where the reverse Greenland model might end up coming in handy. If Brussels and London agree to keep as much of Britain as close as possible to the EU and the single market – that is kind of the normal expectation you have from all these referenda in the Nordic countries: when a political elite wanted something, put it to a referendum and got a 'no', they found a different legal way of achieving something very similar. EngWexit could be the substantial response to receiving a 'no' vote that political leaders did not want. But it is only one of the things that could make for a 'Reverse Greenland' scenario.

Another contributing factor would of course be a credible proposition by the SNP government for a second independence referendum. A third would be if tensions in Northern Ireland were to heat up faced with the prospect of a hard border. Any combination of these, and we might end up in a situation where EU membership proper in these isles was reduced to the periphery, with England and Wales perhaps left in some kind of Norwegian position – possibly glossed over with some reintroduced temporary hand brake on free movement. But we will only really know about that in ten years or so, when negotiations are finished.

The two basic points I want to make are that, first, even if the EU might appear as a very rigid legal community, the political processes that generate EU agreements are chiefly based on pragmatism. So if the UK governments were at some point able to formulate their substantial preferences for what kind of relationship with the EU they want – when the remaining EU governments were given a chance to formulate their preferences – and some kind of compromise is found, then whatever legal and constitutional forms it will take, will be acceptable, at least to the EU. The EU has a habit of being quite flexible and innovative in terms of how to handle sovereignty. If there is a Greenlandic flag as well as a Scottish one, then it does not really make much difference – we are used to juggling sovereignty in weird ways inside the EU.

The second message, I think, that comes out of Greenland's experience, is that it is possible to play games with state sovereignty, and that it can actually be necessary to do so in order to formally uphold it. I think that Lilliput Copenhagen has been slowly learning that over decades. One question is whether London, where memories of imperial grandeur play a more pronounced role, will be able to come to the same kind of conclusion. And then of course it is the reverse question, whether Scotland actually wants to have a pragmatic solution or whether it wants a hard Brexit to help forge a successful independence referendum afterwards.

5

The Faroe Islands – All about Fish

BJØRT SAMUELSEN

FAROE ISLANDS

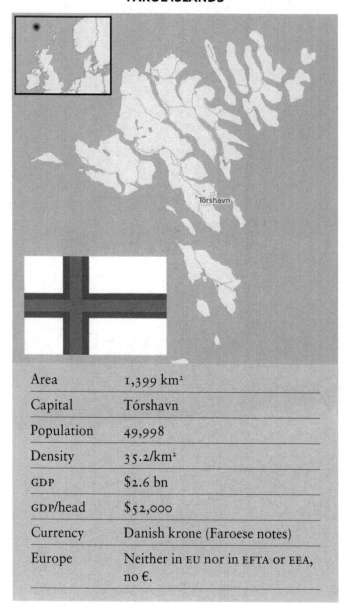

Area	1,399 km²
Capital	Tórshavn
Population	49,998
Density	35.2/km²
GDP	$2.6 bn
GDP/head	$52,000
Currency	Danish krone (Faroese notes)
Europe	Neither in EU nor in EFTA or EEA, no €.

BJØRT SAMUELSEN has something in common with many other
Faroese nationals. She was born in Copenhagen where her
parents were in further education. Bjørt's mother was training
to be a nurse – her dad was studying economics. Back then it
was impossible to study for such professions at home, but in
1965 the opening of the University of the Faroes gradually
changed that. It was the same year Bjørt was born.

The family returned to the Faroes, Bjørt went to school,
worked in France one winter and followed her parents' path to
education abroad and studied Food Science & Technology at
the University of Copenhagen.

> I left school thinking of the Faroes as a fishing country as it had been
> for generations. But in the '80s I thought we should be moving into

an era of higher value products. So, my education was to be able to be help that transition – adding value to what the Faroes already did so well. At the same time, though, I wanted to be a journalist.

When Bjørt went back home, the Faroes (18 rugged islands in the North Atlantic between Shetland and Iceland) were in recession.

It was a very hard time. My husband worked as a vet in our aquaculture industry and he got a job in Norway. So, in 1993 I applied to study journalism in Oslo, Norway, and though I could read Norwegian I had to learn to write and speak the language better – and learn fast. Of course, when you choose another career path later in life, you really focus.

Bjørt and her husband stayed in Norway for eight years during which time their two children were born. She started working for a consumer magazine, then a consumer programme on NRK – Norwegian State Broadcasting. Life was pleasant and easy – why did they opt to go home?

The Faroes were facing exciting times. The Government had called an independence referendum for 2001, so we moved back in November 2000. I thought, I can't be sitting in Norway while such historical things are going on at home. And my oldest daughter was in her first class at school – if she was going to learn Faroese properly we needed to act quickly.

That referendum however, did not take place. 'There was a big crisis in government, so the vote was postponed – and we are still waiting.'

Bjørt started work as a journalist on radio and TV news in the Faroes, which meant closely following politics. After three years, she started her own small journalist and advising company. Then she was recruited as press secretary for the Prime Minister and, in 2007, she took the plunge and decided to go into politics:

I had never wanted to do that before because I believe journalism is one of the most important jobs. But the Faroes was a very male-dominated, patriarchal society and I knew that had to change. The first two women became elected MPs in the Faroese Parliament as late as 1978. We thought numbers would increase with time. In 2002, five of the 32 MPs were women – but at the next election it went back to just three.

Bjørt was running a programme to encourage women to stand and finally decided to take a spoonful of her own medicine, becoming a Republican Party member of the Faroese Parliament in 2008. She was the first female minister of trade and infrastructure until that government lost power and, together with female MPs from two other parties, submitted a same-sex marriage bill which was passed in April 2016.

Scotland's population is 108 times bigger than the Faroe Islands. And while this seafaring nation has sizeable resources of sheep and fish, it has no commercial oil or coal deposits. Still, the Faroese are determined to become economically independent so they can go the extra mile with full political independence when the time is right. That is why the sovereignty-government, led by the Faroese Conservative party, and which the Republican party was part of in 2002, handed back one-third of the block grant from Copenhagen. Yip – you read that right. The Faroese parliament voted to cut the money it receives from the Danish government to wean itself off economic dependence. It is another reason Bjørt decided to join the Republican Party in 2007:

I had wondered which party to run for because I wasn't raised in a party. My family backed the spirit of independence but weren't politically active. But I've always believed taking responsibility is most important – in health, the economy, in language etc. When I look at history, a willingness to take responsibility is what has moved the Faroes forward.

My grandparents all lived till they were almost 100 years old. They were all taught Danish at school in the Faroes – they had to read and write in Danish and back then it wasn't allowed to teach or preach in Faroese at church. Today Faroese is our principal language, we learn Danish only as second language in school. This struggle for our language wouldn't have happened without our sovereignty movement. I'm not so naïve as to think the Faroes can manage completely on our own. We look set to hit the 50,000 population mark in March 2017 but we are still very small. We know we live in an interdependent world. But the three countries within the state of Denmark are not equal. That's why it's very important for us to get a Faroese constitution, confirming the right of the Faroese people to self-determination as well as to take control of foreign policy and other areas of crucial importance.

And to do that the Republicans are prepared to give up the two seats Faroe Islands have in the Danish Parliament: 'Why bother going to Copenhagen if we have taken over all the big issues here? The most important task is for the Faroes to get more economically independent so we get closer to taking total political responsibility too.'

And her thoughts on Scotland?

It's exciting to re-establish old links. Faroese and Scots fisherman are not happy over mackerel and herring quotas but we once had a close relationship. We used to be connected by ferry. At the moment, the main part of our supplies comes from Denmark, even though it's closer and cheaper to get food from Scotland. So that could change. Scottish expertise in green energy is a big area of interest for us, as we have set ambitious green-energy goals, and our telecoms expertise could easily be exported to the Highlands and Islands of Scotland. There's a new Loganair flight from Aberdeen linking Scotland and the Faroes besides the Atlantic Airways route between the Faroe Islands and Edinburgh – so we should explore what we have in common. It's a lot and there is the will to do this.

BEING A NON-EU country in an EU member state, the Faroe Islands are a little country with an interesting relationship to the EU. The population is small, but growing – it is expected to soon pass the 50,000 mark. Some 20,000 live in the capital, Tórshavn. The devolved parliament, Løgtingið, has 33 elected members. The Danish governor general can take seat and speak but has no voting rights. The Faroese Ting has a long tradition – reaching back for over 1,000 years. The modern Løgtingið was established in 1852, as an advisory body. It gained legislative powers when Home Rule was introduced in 1948.

The Faroe Islands may be a small country but, if you look at the Faroese sea area, with 275,000 km² it is not that small. And, with two sub-sea tunnels connecting the islands and two more in progress, it is justly proud of its infrastructure: an efficient, small country with a high living standard. Faroese, the language spoken in the islands, is much closer to Icelandic than to Danish. The country has its own flag – Merkið – thanks to Britain, because during the Second World War Faroese fishing vessels were not allowed to sail under the Danish flag while Denmark was occupied by the Germans and the Faroes were occupied by the British. That circumstance gave the Faroese their own flag.

Not only do the Faroese have their own Parliament, they also have a national football team (as Scots knows only too well). You will hear about pilot whaling which is one of our ways to supply food. We also like to come together and chain dance and sing hymns. Especially during the Ólavsøka, the national day and big summer festival in the Faroe Islands, which features our national sport: rowing.

Who is Faroese? That is quite an interesting question. The Faroe Islands are a self-governing nation under the sovereignty of the Kingdom of Denmark. So, all Faroese are born Danish citizens, but they must be resident – present or former – in the Faroe Islands in order to be regarded as Faroese.

The Faroese make a living from the sea. We have fishing and aquaculture, and fish products are our biggest export – 94 per cent of all our exports of goods. Half of that is salmon. We also have tourism, which is growing, not as fast as in Iceland, but interest in visiting the Nordic countries has increased and that includes exploring the further north, like the Faroe Islands. We have shipping and offshore services, and like to call ourselves a maritime service hub. We have growing cultural and creative industries. And we have some agriculture and food production.

The Faroese Parliament is the parliament of a self-governing country and so has exclusive competence to legislate and govern independently over a wide range of areas. Fiscal and tax legislation is extremely important because we can decide how to use our money and how to collect taxes, and how much tax we levy. We also have industrial and business legislation, but cannot regulate the banks; that is Denmark's responsibility. The management of fisheries is, next to fiscal and tax legislation, the most important devolved responsibility. We are also fully autonomous with regard to energy policy. All natural resources, including sub-surface resources like oil or gas, are within our legislative remit. Of course, we are not an oil-producing country, not yet, but it is very important for us that we have won those rights. We did not always have them, but we fiercely struggled to get them, and succeeded in the end to persuade the Danes to transfer the juridical competence, which they used to say was impossible due to the Danish constitution.

The Danish Parliament, though, still retains quite a few legislation rights over Faroese matters. But, Danish legislation can only come into force if and when it has been ratified by the Faroese authorities. And that is why you will often see 'This Act does not apply to the Faroes' or 'to the Faroes and Greenland' attached to Danish laws made by the Danish Parliament, the Folketing, if they are not ratified by the Løgting or Greenland's Landsting.

We can unilaterally decide to transfer powers from Denmark, except in the following areas, which are more complicated: the Danish state constitution, citizenship, the Supreme Court, foreign policy, security and defence policy, and the currency.

Most areas concerning the everyday life of the Faroese are within the competency of Faroese authorities, and we could take control of our prisons, civil aviation, passport office and police, family and inheritance law, and immigration and border control. We are working on some of them. The next area to be transferred to the Faroese authorities will be family and inheritance law, and we are also working on immigration and border control. Of course, we would like to control who can come to the Faroe Islands and not be delayed by a strict and bureaucratic Danish system.

The Faroe Islands are neither a member of the European Union nor of the European Economic area. The country is seeking EFTA (European Free Trade Association) membership, which it has aspired to for many years. It would like to join Norway, Iceland, Switzerland and Liechtenstein in EFTA. Furthermore, the Faroes are not one of the OCTs (Overseas Country and Territories) as Greenland is, which means that Greenland has a totally different status relating to the EU. There are EU countries, EEA countries, and Greenland as an OCT – the Faroes are 'none of the above'.

As already indicated, the Faroe Islands are not independent regarding foreign relations. Foreign matters are under the control of Denmark, so when it comes to foreign policy there are a range of things we cannot decide. But we do negotiate our own fisheries policy and participate in several international fishery management arrangements.

That could be NAMMCO (North Atlantic Marine Mammal Commission), concerning whales, or our associate memberships in United Nations agencies like FAO (Food and Agriculture Organisation), IMO (International Maritime Organisation) and UNESCO.

We also have built up international representations over the last decades We have representative offices in Brussels and London, Copenhagen and Reykjavik, and we recently opened one in Moscow. We are aiming at adding representations – USA and/or China might be next. There probably should be one in Edinburgh, too. We used to have a representative in Aberdeen. Though the representative offices cannot be called embassies, they are very important for Faroese foreign and business policy.

To understand the present situation of the Faroe Islands, we need to get a grasp of history, without which the differences between Denmark and the Faroes, and their respective relationships with the EU, cannot be understood. Following the 1814 Peace Treaty of Kiel, the Faroe Islands ceased to be part of Norway (Denmark–Norway Kingdom) and became an overseas colony or protectorate under the Danish Crown. In 1816 the Faroese Parliament, one of the oldest in the word, was abolished, along with the position of the prime minister (Løgmaður), and the islands became a Danish county, or 'amt', and the Parliament was only re-established in 1852. Not as a real, decision-making parliament, but only as a consultative body advising the Danish government. The chief administrative officer of Denmark (Amtmaður) was the head of the Faroese Parliament. So, the parliament representing the Faroese people was controlled by a Danish civil servant.

This was of course not a happy situation. When, during

the Second World War the Faroe Islands were occupied by the British and Denmark by the Germans, the connection between Denmark and the Faroe Islands was cut. We were in much closer contact with the UK during the Second World War and that did change minds. The Faroe Islands lost a lot of seamen during the war, daily putting their lives at jeopardy by sailing fish to supply the UK market, but at the same time the country's wealth was growing. We had a lot of Pounds sterling in British banks. Denmark seemed further and further away. And when Iceland got its independence in 1944 – which few saw coming since there were only 130,000 Icelanders at that time – that was a big boost to the Faroese independence movement.

An independence referendum was held in 1946 in the Faroe Islands. The Danes were absolutely sure that the Faroese people were going to say no. People could choose between a very narrow Home Rule Act or total independence, so for many it was a very difficult choice. But the Faroese people chose yes to independence, and although it was by a small majority, it was a clear yes. That came as a surprise to both the Danes and the unionist movement on the Islands. They would not have imagined that the majority would say yes. But they did. Undoubtedly inspired by the fact that the Faroes had managed perfectly well without Denmark during years of war, the country had even grown richer, and if the Icelanders could, why shouldn't we be able to stand on own feet?

To cut a very long story short, we did not get independence. The will of the people was over-ruled. A general election was held which returned a Unionist majority. What we got was the Home Rule Act of 1948. And with that, the Faroese Parliament got legislative powers. The Home Rule Act was amended in 2005.

Denmark applied for membership of the EEC back in

1961. At that time, following a very difficult decision by the Faroese Parliament, the Faroes would have joined along with Denmark. Not because they wanted to, but because the Faroese parliamentarians were afraid to stand outside both EFTA and EEC/EU since those were our biggest fish export markets. Though, the decision would have to be put to the Parliament once more for a final decision, if or when a Danish membership became reality.

But, in the course of the next decade or so, scepticism grew quickly. The Faroese people had always been sceptical of the EEC, because they were afraid of losing the right to decide their own fishing policy. This developed into a people's movement, led by the charismatic leader of Tjóðveldi (the Republican or Independence Party), Mr Erlendur Patursson. There were demonstrations in the streets in the early 1970s shouting 'EEC against the people/the people against the EEC'. Thus, the people's movement spoke very strongly against the Faroe Islands joining the European Community.

What was that all about? Why were people in the Faroe Islands against joining the EEC? There is a very simple answer to that question: fish. Fish and the right to control your own fishing policy. The Faroe Islanders were terrified, especially the fishermen, that the British and the Germans, Italians and Spanish would enter our sea area and fish into our rocky coast. We had struggled to get control of our 12-mile exclusive fishing zone, and were fighting on to win control of our 200-mile exclusive zone (which we succeeded in 1977) – and were very much afraid of putting that in jeopardy. The Parliament's 1961 decision did not get a hearing in 1972 – and the result was that we did not enter the EEC together with Denmark in 1973.

Denmark initially tried to make us join. But they very quickly found out that it would not be sensible to force the Faroe Islands, as a fishing community, into the EEC. And my personal view is that Denmark was also afraid to again 'wake up the giant' that was moving towards independence. So, Denmark supported the will of the Faroe Islands to stay outside. A special arrangement was made for us to decide whether to join or not. The Faroese were given two years to answer – but after one year they told Denmark that they had definitely decided to stay outside. And that is still the case: a huge majority wants to stay outside the EU.

What is the advantage for a country of 50,000 people being out there and outside, quite alone sometimes? There are some advantages. We do control our own fishing policy which is so important for us. We do not have to implement all those rules and laws implemented in EU countries. And that is often a good thing. But, anyway, we still try to harmonise our laws because it is difficult to do business with other countries if we do not have laws that are compatible. It is much easier to cooperate with your neighbours if your law system and the law you have implemented are quite alike.

Sometimes it can be very harsh being small and up against a giant –which the EU definitely is – as well as nearly everyone else, compared to us. A prime example occurred in 2013, when the EU, including Denmark, imposed sanctions on the Faroe Islands as a result of a dispute regarding the coastal state negotiations on Atlanto-Scandian herring. They imposed an embargo on Faroese fishing vessels as well as imports of herring and mackerel products from the Faroes. Fishing vessels were not allowed to enter any harbour in the EU and neither were the mentioned fish products. So, we were boycotted by Denmark, even though we are regarded as being a part of the Danish Kingdom. A very peculiar situation indeed.

Another disadvantage is that it can often be very hard to get a good deal when you are outside. You do not have many allies who can help you to get what you want. Few want to put a lot of effort into something one single country wants, particularly if that country has chosen to stay outside the club.

As mentioned, Denmark is a member state of the European Union, but the EU treaties do not apply to the Faroe Islands. Accordingly, the Faroes negotiate their own trade and fisheries agreements with the EU and other countries.

We have a fisheries agreement with the EU. We also have a Free Trade agreement. It covers all industrial goods with limitations for agricultural and fisheries products. The fishery products which can be exported without tariffs to the EU market are listed on a so-called positive list. This agreement is a good one, though we are trying to extend it. But that's not the end of our ambitions. We also strive to improve our association with the EU on innovation and research, and are now an associated country in Horizon 2020.

We have a taskforce evaluating options and priorities for modernising our relationship with the EU, and we would very much like the EU to do the same – meaning an EU body to handle Faroese issues due to options and priorities for modernising the relationship. We would also like better EU recognition of the Faroe Islands as a European third country and partner.

We do want better access to the single market for processed fish and products and in other areas. Not having that means having to find partners elsewhere to deal with. I could mention Russia and China, to whom we have a substantial export to today.

The Faroese government is, as mentioned above, aiming strongly at membership of EFTA. That is quite difficult to attain. We put great effort in it, and hope to succeed in a not too distant future. We also would like to gain full membership of the World Trade Organisation (WTO) – and we want full membership of the Nordic Council. We are also working on a constitution for the Faroes, which we have been working on for ten or more years. A referendum on the proposed constitution is scheduled for 2018.

The case of the Faroe Islands shows, to a certain degree, that where there is a will there is a way to find pragmatic solutions. However, it takes a lot of effort and time, and – to a great extent – is dependent on the goodwill of all parties involved.

I know that Scotland and the UK are facing a challenging situation after the Brexit vote. In addition to the Faroese case, it might be worth mentioning that, as I understand, the EU is currently working on a special arrangement for small countries – small states like Monaco, San Marino, Andorra – meaning it is open to differentiated relationships. In the end, it is important to find solutions that respect the will of the people concerned. In the case of the Scottish people, it seems obvious that they do not want to leave the EU.

6

Fishing, Forestry and Agriculture: Sustainability and the 'Norwegian Model'

DUNCAN HALLEY

NORWAY

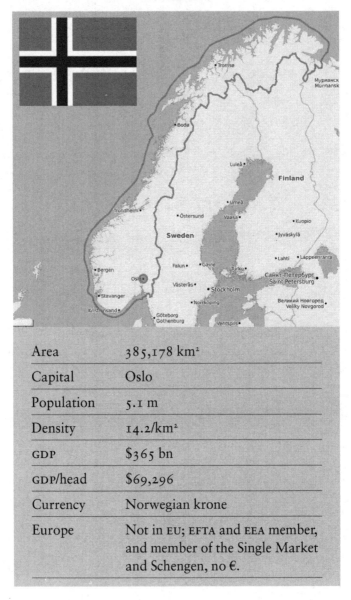

Area	385,178 km²
Capital	Oslo
Population	5.1 m
Density	14.2/km²
GDP	$365 bn
GDP/head	$69,296
Currency	Norwegian krone
Europe	Not in EU; EFTA and EEA member, and member of the Single Market and Schengen, no €.

6

DUNCAN HALLEY used to be Scottish. To be more precise, he used to be a resident of Scotland and thus a citizen of the UK until the logic of work and the abundance of wildlife took him to Norway in 1993. Fifteen years later, the Dundee lad formally became a Norwegian citizen. 'It was strangely uneventful. I just took a piece of paper to the police station, signed something and got a Norwegian passport 20 minutes later.'

But why? From an early age Duncan was interested in birds and wildlife. As a child he remembers feeding birds throughout the winter – nothing unusual about that except Duncan wanted to know where those birds went next and joined Dundee Young Ornithologists as a teenager. Duncan's first hike away from the safety and familiarity of roads was a hike through Glen Doll at the age of 14 as part of the Duke of Edinburgh award scheme. Thus the two great loves of his life were cemented together and bird-watching in the Great Outdoors blossomed into a long career studying animal behaviour across the world. But not from the vantage point of Scotland

Studying at St Andrews was a big culture shock. It was just 12 miles from Dundee but there was a big percentage of folk from the south of England and public school and some of them had, to the Dundee lad, bizarre social attitudes.

> I got very used to being asked what my dad did, and how I phrased my reply affecting how I was regarded. My PhD there was meant to be a study of the behaviour and ecology of buzzards using radio telemetry but we couldn't catch enough to tag, so instead I studied guillemots on the Isle of May. It was far easier. There are 40 pairs per square metre on cliff ledges there – it's the densest breeding environment for birds in the world.

And then came Norway. A year in Trondheim was all it took. Duncan travelled there after doing a PhD in Zoology at St Andrews University. He wanted to find out whether sea eagles or golden eagles were the more dominant species and could only do that in a place with fully developed populations of both living together. Norway was the only place on earth with both sea eagles and a similar climate to Scotland.

Duncan's work was considered sufficiently important to win funding by the British Royal Society, but the main issue was settled in a week. Even amateur ornithologists in Norway already knew the answer. Golden eagles are dominant even though they are physically smaller because they are faster and meaner. It was a revelation.

> Across all sorts of issues – animal behaviour, wildlife habitats, land and marine management – what was not known was often already known by the Norwegians. Just as often, things we in Scotland

assumed were just naturally so, turned out not to be – facts on the ground in Norway disproved them. As I looked round I found that was true at a social level too. Things considered impossible in Scotland were actually and easily happening here.

It had been a relatively easy decision to leave Scotland – but it was a bigger decision to stay in Norway.

Duncan has a penchant for rattling out statistics and a knack of capturing difficult arguments with succinct comparisons. That was what staggered the audience at Nordic Horizons in 2015 when he demonstrated beyond any doubt that the apparently barren, treeless nature of the Highlands could be like the naturally regenerated fjord and fjell of South West Norway.

Why is Norway so much better as a place to live?

Norwegians as individuals are not cleverer or nicer than Scots or anyone else. There are a few reasons for their success – above all they had some luck and were able to run with the ball they were given, entering the twentieth century with a fairly equal, flat society. The Second World War was a very uniting experience that left Norwegians determined to get rid of any remaining social unfairness. I'm a Scot born and bred, so I'm not prone to gushing. Let's say, Norway is not Nirvana – it's simply the least worst society in the world. Not necessarily the happiest, but this country will not give you a hard time just because you have been unlucky with the cards you are dealt in life.

Interestingly, that enlightened attitude contributed materially to Duncan's decision to stay. Norwegian law dictates that anyone casually employed by the same company for more than three years can request to be made a full-time staff member instead, with all the generous rights and allowances a permanent job brings. It seems that law was brought in decades back to stop casualisation of the Norwegian workforce and deter employers from trying to get around new maternity and paternity allowances. After five changes of administration, and despite a Conservative government now, that law has not been changed.

In Scotland, it is doubtful a wildlife researcher like Duncan would have had the same security and continuity of employment. He's taken on and helped win contracts with the same employers (NINA – The Norwegian Institute for Nature Research) for the last 23 years.

A lot of Duncan's work has been in central Europe – especially Slovenia and Romania – thanks to an EEA programme that replicates EU funding for less favoured areas. Norway provides 96 per cent of the cash for practical programmes like research on ecosystem services in Romania.

What's that? 'Studying things nature gives us for free because in today's world if we don't put a price tag on them we'll probably trash them.'

He has also studied the grazing ecology of sheep and reindeer in Norway, was part of the team reintroducing sea eagles from Norway to Ireland, and over many years advised on beaver reintroduction and management in Scotland.

Duncan met his Japanese wife, Sachiko Shin, at St Andrews when he was doing his PhD. They worked in different countries until she left her job to go to Trondheim and get married in 1999. The couple had a son the same year, after which Sachiko got a job teaching Japanese at the Norwegian University for Science and Technology.

Does Duncan miss Scotland?

Scotland is sometimes a bit parochial for a place that thinks it is outward looking. Lots of Norwegian experience is hugely relevant to Scotland, but until now many Scots have seen themselves unconsciously as inhabitants of a peninsula north of the world, as it were. It's particularly daft that the Scottish Civil Service is in practice banned from visiting eg Norway in case their trip looks like a jolly. But trips within the UK are allowed, so the civil servant's main point of reference is still England. That's perverse on a number of levels.

Seeing is believing. I remember a guy from a Scottish landowning charity who believed that upper Glen Affric was naturally treeless. I took him to a glen just like it near Stavanger, though with an even worse climate, that was covered in trees that had naturally regenerated. His jaw dropped.

If I had millions I'd set up a foundation to get folk from Scotland over here.

Without winning the lottery though, Duncan's contribution to the Nordic Brexit event prompted Alex Salmond and two other MPs to travel to Oslo for a meeting with Duncan about the potential benefits of Scottish control of fishery and agricultural policy and aiming to get more productivity from Scotland's natural assets.

THE NORWEGIAN INSTITUTE for Nature Research (NINA) for which I work is not a government agency. It is more like the Centre for Ecology and Hydrology, or the James Hutton Institute in what it does. So looking at Norway, I want to slightly narrow the focus. One of the few things that is pretty much clear about Brexit is that whether it is hard or whether it is soft, it is going to bring fisheries and land use down to much greater control at the Scottish level.

In Norway – which is not a member of the EU – these things have always been managed by our Parliament and not by the Common Fisheries Policy or Common Agricultural Policy. So I want to look at how that works for Norway and to suggest there might be opportunities for Scotland, given that it seems very likely Scotland will be spending at least some time not fully integrated into EU institutions. But before we go any further, we should take a brief look at Norway's relationship to the European Union.

When, in 2005, the French and Dutch voted 'No' to the proposed European constitution, the polls in Norway shifted quite strongly overnight and, since then, they have never been close to backing a Norwegian bid to join the EU. The Lisbon Treaty of 2007 was perceived by many in Norway as a threat to democracy – and Norwegians are keen on their local democracy. So that does appear to have had a further negative effect. Then came the Greek debt crisis.

Now, the polls indicate that more than 70 per cent of Norwegians are against joining; less than 20 per cent are in favour; and around ten per cent are in the don't know bracket. Neither the more recent Syrian migrant crisis nor the Brexit referendum in the UK seem to have had any effect, and the Norwegian equivalent of polling expert John Curtice, a guy called Øyvind Østerud, said we have now probably reached the bedrock of 'yes' supporters and that support for EU membership could not go any lower.

About the only group in the whole of Norway that is still about evenly split on EU membership is the demographic of career politicians. Every other demographic is not in favour. The younger you are, the more you are against joining the EU. Also, generally speaking, people on the political left tend to be more against joining than people on the political right.

Instead, Norway is a member of the European Economic Area (EEA). Membership was agreed in 1992, ahead of the 1994 EU referendum, and came into force from the beginning of 1994. Joining the EEA was intended by the Norwegian Government as a stepping stone on the way to full EU. But in a referendum every bit as bizarre and confrontational as the British one, Norwegians rejected EU membership by 52 to 48 per cent; as they had once before, in 1972. Membership remained a live issue through to 2005. Plans for a third referendum were dropped then, not just because the timing would have meant it coincided with the centenary of Norway's independence, but because there was no realistic prospect of a 'yes' vote.

It's worth noting that Norwegians have a long history of helping to found and working with European and world institutions in general; and under the EEA deal there are more immigrants from EU countries per capita than Britain, without it being an issue in Norway. 'Little Norwayism' has not been a large factor in debates over EU membership.

The current political debate centres on the EEA deal: whether it is a good one, whether it should be continued or replaced. But those considerations are now on hold until it becomes clear what Brexit actually means for the UK, because that is likely to change the political landscape in which Norway operates.

The EEA agreement essentially means membership of the single market. It provides for the inclusion into Norwegian law of EU legislation on free movement of goods, services, persons and capital. The agreement requires equal rights and obligations within the internal market. It means we apply the majority of EU directives and regulations. But – and I have not seen this mentioned in British discussions – there is a thing called the right of reservation. Any country can invoke it, and it then suspends a directive indefinitely from applying to the EEA only countries – Norway, Iceland and Liechtenstein. It has only been used once so far, by the Norwegian centre-left coalition in 2011 on the postal directive, because of the implications they feared it had for rural areas. But that was reversed by the current minority right coalition in 2013.

Importantly, the EEA agreement does not include the following EU policy areas: the Common Fisheries Policy, the Common Agricultural Policy – I will talk about these two in greater detail – as well as the Habitat Directive, the Conservation Directive, the Customs Union, the Common Trade Policy, Common Foreign and Security policy, justice and home affairs and the monetary union. In any form of Brexit, it can be expected that all of these would go back into the remit of the UK or Scotland.

Post Brexit – at least according to the Scotland Act 1998 which puts fisheries clearly into the Scottish domain – all fishing policy and management currently done at EU level would move to be controlled by the Scottish Parliament. The Scottish Exclusive Economic Zone is about 56 per cent of the size of Norway's. The big question is sustainability of fish stocks. Back in the 1960s and '70s, when fishing stocks collapsed because of technological improvements, we did not really know how to manage them sustainably – but now we do. We know how to fish sustainably. It may be relatively complex but, to put it simply, you collect certain data, you put them into the spreadsheet, and it tells you how many fish you can catch. And then it is a matter of whether we have the political will to act accordingly.

So what does the EU itself say about its own policies? Its

6

Reform Green Paper from 2009 says that most stocks have been fished down. Eighty-eight per cent of stocks are fished beyond maximum sustainable yield. Thirty per cent are outside safe biological limits. That means they are at risk of extinction. Ninety-three per cent of cod in the North Sea are fished before they can breed. And there is a heavy financial burden on the public purse. European citizens must pay for their fish twice – once in the shop and then again through their taxes. The EU Fisheries Commissioner has said: 'If no reform takes place, only eight stocks out of 136 will be at sustainable levels in 2022.'

Professor Orbach is a fisheries lawyer based at Tromsø University who has studied the subject. In the entire North Sea, out of 18 stocks, nine are not fishable at all. Of the remaining species all nine were heavily reduced between 1997 and 2009. By this he means they remained at a much lower level than their biological capacity, not that the population actually declined during that period. The latest reform has been phased in since 2015. Maybe it will work. At the moment, however, there appears to be some doubt about this.

Fixing the level of fish quotas that can be caught is a complex process. Sometimes scientific advice on how much of a certain species should be caught is followed to the letter, but it is not unusual for ministers to set levels that are very different. The effect of that is that in the Northeast Atlantic/ North Sea/ Baltic, well over half of the slightly more than 50 regional fish stocks are outside safe biological limits. The region accounts for 74 per cent of the total EU catch. In 2015, the proportion of Scotland's key commercial stocks in line with scientific guidance was 57 per cent. That is above average for the EU. But Scotland still puts 43 per cent of its stocks outside of what the scientists say is defensible.

So far – and it is really too early to tell – the outcome of

CFP reforms does not look all that good. The policy was to remedy the Common Fisheries Policy's 'five structural failings'. Unfortunately, the new regulations have failed to improve the situation. No radical changes have taken place. It remains to be seen whether the new regime can work.

In fact, since 2000, Scotland saw a six per cent increase in the value of all landings. We are talking about money now. Demersal – that means bottom living stocks – have declined, the others have slightly increased, but overall it is pretty flat, at an already low level. And the subsidies do not come cheap. For the Scottish sector, they amounted to £101.8 million in direct subsidies between 2007 and 2014. That did not include 'other government contributions' – I have been unable to locate what those are – or indirect subsidies. The biggest indirect subsidy is exemption from fuel taxes – a very large subsidy indeed. The new EU fisheries programme, which started operating in 2015, includes a replacement for this fund. It covers the period between 2015 and 2020. It will provide €6.4bn in subsidies – 27 per cent for 'sustainable fisheries'.

Now, let us turn to Norway. I was hoping I could be more nuanced and 'balanced' on this matter but the data, I am afraid, just does not support it. Here are some verdicts on the Norwegian fisheries policy:

'State of the most important commercial fish stocks is good,' says the OECD. 'The Norwegian management of living material marine resources is based on the best available scientific evidence,' according to the UN's Food and Agriculture Organisation. And, most succinctly, the Marine Stewardship Council: 'Norwegian fisheries management is simply world class.'

Fisheries fulfil a number of roles in Norway. The first one is with regard to society. It is the backbone of coastal Norway. If fishing went out of business, pretty much all the rural communities would just pack up overnight. It is of vital importance to settlement and employment. The seafood industry generates great value. It is Norway's second biggest export, after oil and gas. And we also want to manage it in a way that is appropriate for the environment.

Norway makes $8.9bn (£5.3bn) a year out of seafood products – about equally split between aquaculture and actual fishing. Seafood is our second-most important export item; 90 per cent of all seafood products are exported. 73.6 per cent of the fish caught are from certified stocks, the highest proportion in the world. We manage this through the Marine Resources Act. The purpose of the law is to ensure sustainable and socio-economically profitable management of marine resources.

In addition, there is the Participation Act which stipulates that fishing boats must be owned by registered fishermen active on the boat, or administering it on land – that allows for older fishermen to retire from active fishing, while continuing employment associated with the boat. If owned by a company, the company must be owned by active fishermen working on the boat or in its administration. A dispensation may be granted so that fish processing firms can own up to 49.9 per cent, but the controlling interest has to be active fishermen, people who actually are out there on the sea doing the job. And, finally, the fish is sold through sales organisations which are cooperatives owned by the fishermen.

The system is overseen by the Director of Fisheries. Norway has banned discard for many years now, as a waste of resources. They are also not registered in the statistics, and that makes it hard for researchers to actually calculate the state of the stocks.

In the 1970s there was an over-fishing crisis in Norway due to the development of new technologies. Many stocks collapsed and (as in the EU) large amounts of money were ploughed into the sector to prevent bankruptcies and prevent depopulation of rural communities.

Reforms were then made, resulting in the management structure we see today. The effect of Norway's fisheries policy reform has been that, between 1985 and 2015, the spawning stock of pelagic (open water) fish species has increased by 51 per cent; and the spawning stock of demersal (bottom-living) fish species has increased by 340 per cent. Thus, since we took our management under proper control, the size of our resource has increased very considerably.

At the same time, the size of our subsidy has dropped to almost zero. All that remains is participation in a number of general industrial subsidies, eg for training courses and so forth, which are not really aimed at fisheries exclusively. You might also call the exemption from the carbon dioxide and sulphur dioxide levies that we have on fuel in Norway a subsidy; but I do not think these levies exist in Britain. VAT for fuel has to be paid. As to monetary values of landings, Norway saw a 40 per cent increase during the period from 2000 to 2015 – compared to 6 per cent in the Scottish sector.

But it could be even better than that. The most important fish stocks migrate between Norwegian and foreign waters and, consequently, good governance requires close cooperation with neighbouring countries. In the North Sea both cod and haddock stocks are stable but at very low levels. And the population of saithe (pollock) has been declining.

Multilateral cooperation in this area is organised through the Northeast Atlantic Fisheries Cooperation (NEAFC), comprising the EU, Russia, Norway, the Faroe Islands, and Denmark (representing Greenland). So, how is the Northeast Atlantic Fishery doing? Back in 2009, only the Norwegian Spring herring stock was considered sustainable.

If you look at the NEAFC scientific minutes for 2015, data was still missing from both Greenland and the EU on deep sea fisheries. As the minutes note, 'given the extent of their fisheries, the EU data was particularly important. It served little purpose to carry on the exercise without it'.

NEAFC also had a performance review in 2014. It has not been published yet but, as a result of it, Agenda item 4 – supported by the European Union and the Norwegians – notes the main issue is the failure to agree on comprehensive management measures for several of the most important fish stocks managed by this organisation. There is not much evidence, therefore, to suggest that this multilateral system is working very well.

How about bilateral cooperation, then? We have problems in many areas with Russia, but this is not one of them. In 2008, Norway and Russia instituted a joint management plan for the Norwegian Sea/Barents Sea cod stock, because both sides realised that our economic interests were very much in line on this issue. More stringent quotas were applied. These days it is possible to enforce them; in the early years after the collapse of the Soviet Union that was not the case. Things changed after the new policy came into force in 2008. Fish stocks can recover quickly when managed correctly. By 2010 harvests were already higher than in the period before 2008; by 2013, the cod stock had more than doubled and the measured biomass of fish in the Barents Sea exceeded that of any time in the previous 50 years – in fact, since statistics have been kept.

The Norwegian-Russian cod stock is now the largest cod stock in the world. It is in very good condition, according to Fisheries Norway, the official regulators. In the North Sea, the Norwegian-EU cod stock remains in a very poor condition.

To sum up: The Common Fisheries Policy is subsidised.

Values of Scottish catches have increased by six per cent between 2000 and 2015. EU ministerial meetings frequently overrule scientific advice on sustainable catches. In 2015, 43 per cent of Scottish stocks were not managed according to scientific advice. In contrast, the Norwegian fishing industry is not subsidised. Values of Norwegian catches have increased by 40 per cent over the same period. Seafood is our second-largest export. Our ministers do not overrule scientific advice on catches. Revenues and profits flow through Norwegian coastal communities. Note also that not just the revenues but also the profits flow through Norwegian coastal communities. The stocks are mostly in good condition, and the main exceptions – the data is clear on this – are where they are shared with the EU's Common Fisheries Policy. Social consensus regarding our fisheries system is very high indeed. That is not surprising, it is a conspicuous success.

To its credit, the EU acknowledges that fisheries is an area of serious policy failure – their fisheries people have said so in very clear terms – but the EU's political decision-making process has failed to come up with reforms that seriously address the issue. Whatever you think about the European Union in general, on this particular issue there is a lot of room for improvement.

And what about the future? For the Norwegians, cooperation with Russia is good and stocks are doing very well. The Norwegians are making money, and the Russians are making money. Cooperation with the EU is problematic because of overfishing. Many of those 43 per cent of stocks that are not being managed sustainably inside the Scottish sector are shared with Norway, particularly important stocks like North Sea cod. So for the Norwegians, the prospect of Scotland controlling its own fisheries from 2019 is seen as a considerable opportunity. It is also, I think, a considerable opportunity for the Scots. But only, and this needs to be emphasised, if stocks are managed properly and not politically. It is perfectly possible to damage your stocks alone. You remember the phrase about the Barents Sea having the largest cod stock in the world. That title used to belong to the Grand Banks fishery off Newfoundland, Canada; but they destroyed their stock by 1994 all by themselves.

So the point is, the politicians need to listen to what the scientists say, and they will have to face down short term opposition from their domestic fishing industry – and you can be sure of that opposition because it will mean their profits will take a hit, at least for a year or two. But if you persevere, the gains are high. The gains for Norway would be high as well.

Let me turn to the issue of rural communities, farming and forestry. The picture in Norway has dramatically changed over the past hundred years or so. A lot of forest has been planted. More has grown back by natural regeneration. And land has been converted to arable. There is no intrinsic reason why many areas of the Highlands of Scotland could not undergo a similar transformation.

The projected payments through the Common Agricultural Policy (CAP) of the EU to Scotland for 2015 to 2020 amount to £4.6bn. Most of that huge sum goes on direct payments, that means paying farmers per area of land, or paying them for having sheep, for example. The rest goes on rural development through less favoured area grants, agricultural environment schemes, forestry grants, and the like.

When CAP was devised in 1962, it was intended to support rural communities. But it was devised in the context of the European Six, and particularly for the interests of small farmers in Italy and France. Most people in those communities were small owner-occupier farmers and their families, while Scotland has an ownership pattern of agricultural land that is at the opposite extreme. Most farms in Scotland are very large – over two square kilometres in extent.

Projected direct payments through the current scheme are £176 per hectare for arable and improved grazing, £28 for better quality rough grazing and £8 for poorer quality rough grazing, plus headage payments for sheep: £77 at current exchange rates per ewe on rough grazing, and £73 for beef cattle calves on the mainland, £117 on the islands.

Norwegian farms, by contrast, are generally very small, a few hectares of arable land plus a bit of hill area. They are nearly always family farms and must be owned by an individual. Nearly all our forest is associated with these farms. Our forestry is dominated by areas owned by the farmers themselves. And they are used for things beyond the production of timber: for fuel harvesting, hunting, grazing, and so on. Nearly all of it is owned by people that live locally. There is no real Norwegian equivalent of the Forestry Commission. Take Orkdal, a typical *kommune* (local government district; places like Atholl or Lorne would be *kommunes* if there was the same system in Scotland) near where I live. Seventy-eight per cent of the forest resource is owned by individuals resident in that district and most of the land is used for farming and forestry. Some may be used for farming only, some for forestry only but, generally, our farming and forestry are tightly mixed.

In most cases, the farmer who owns the property lives there. To inherit a farm, you must undertake to live there, use it as your main residence, and work it for five years. If you want to buy one, you have to commit to that for ten years. That is to prevent places from being turned into summer homes, or for them being bought up by people who live in cities or outside Norway and who do not intend to settle there – thus weakening the rural community socially and financially.

The principal goals of agricultural policy are safeguarding food supply at a reasonable price, preserving distinctive features of the Norwegian rural landscape, and guaranteeing the viability of rural communities. Twice in the last century, during both World Wars, Norway had to feed itself. Cheap food for 30 years is great, but we would starve to death in the 31st year if international supply chains – and we are at the end of those chains – were to be blocked. Supermarkets in Norway and Scotland may not look much different, but the proportion of locally grown food is much higher.

Farmers' markets in Norway, catering to the local/slow food market, are an increasing feature in the overall food market. For example, the Christmas Farmers' Market in Trondheim occupies a tent that runs about 300 metres along the road. Hundreds of farms are represented there. Often customers develop a relationship with a particular farmer whose products they enjoy, adding a social dimension to the purely commercial transaction.

Average income from land use is £21,000 from the farm, though total income for the average farmer is £51,000, because the farmer often works outside the farm. That compares with £16,000 for an average farm worker in Scotland, or £31,000 for an actual farmer – ie tenant farmers or owner-occupiers farming themselves. It also means that rural population density in the southwest of Norway, which is very similar to the Scottish Highlands in all the relevant factors, is very much higher.

Our agricultural support system cost £1.14bn per year in 2015. That was 1.2 per cent of overall government spending – less than half, incidentally, of what goes into overseas aid. It is probably worth pointing out that if you annualise the CAP payment projections for Scotland they amount to about the same: £1.1bn per year. But also, importantly, Norway's external tariffs are very much higher than Britain's.

Almost all the money that goes through this system flows through land users who are resident in rural communities, underpinning the entire rural economy. They make up 3 per cent of the total population of Norway, and a much higher percentage in rural areas. The money gets spent in the shops, it supports the school because the children go there, it supports the social institutions. And the system overall enjoys relatively broad social consensus.

My point with respect to agriculture is not that Scotland should attempt to reproduce this. Scotland is, in many ways, a very different country. It has got those big mountain areas, but also large areas of high quality arable land. The interest is thus not in reproducing the system as such. The point is that Norway is able to tailor its system to *its* self-defined goals of what it wants from its land. This is much less practicable inside the Common Agricultural Policy.

The CAP will soon cease to apply in Scotland, assuming there is a break in the UK's full membership of the EU, and a new system for rural support farming will have to be legislated for by the Scottish Government. The exception would be that the level of external agricultural tariffs would be set at UK level. This new system does not have to be anything like the Common Agricultural Policy in its structure, its content or scope.

What I am essentially asking are questions which, I suggest, Scots should be asking themselves. What is it you want from your rural community/land use system in the 21st century? How do you structure a system to achieve that? Where should the money flow, how much and to whom? Starting in 2019, it appears you will have pretty much sole control over those questions. The same is true of fisheries policy.

These are complex and important questions – I would suggest it is high time for a great debate.

7

No signs of Swexit
– Sweden and the
European Union

PADDY BORT

SWEDEN

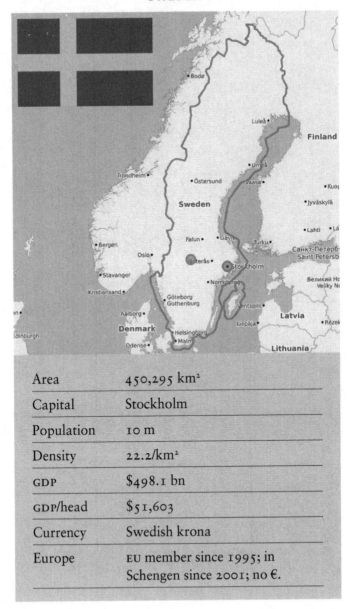

Area	450,295 km²
Capital	Stockholm
Population	10 m
Density	22.2/km²
GDP	$498.1 bn
GDP/head	$51,603
Currency	Swedish krona
Europe	EU member since 1995; in Schengen since 2001; no €.

EBERHARD 'PADDY' BORT was the Convener and Director of
Studies of the Academy of Government's Parliamentary
Internship Programme. His teaching at Edinburgh University
included Scottish Society and Culture, Contemporary Irish
Politics, The Politics of Borders, and British Studies. He was also
Book Reviews Editor of *Scottish Affairs*.

He came to Edinburgh from Tübingen in 1995 on a research
contract – to study the borders of the European Union – which
included the peculiar arrangement in place at that time at the
Finnish-Russian border. His interest in the Nordic countries had
already been kindled when he attended a four-day conference
in Trondheim in the early 1990s. At Edinburgh University, he
helped to coordinate a series of visits by Danish English

teachers to Scotland, and was invited to be a guest teacher at a Gymnasium in Copenhagen.

> For a week, I visited classes at the Jespersen Gymnasium, talking about Scotland and its relationship to the Nordic countries. And here was time to explore the cultural life of the Danish capital, as well as visits to Roskilde and to the famous Louisiana Museum of Modern Art.

Before coming to Edinburgh in 1995, Paddy worked at Tübingen University in British and Irish Studies with Professor Christopher Harvie and taught German Studies at Trinity College, Dublin, and at the University of Puget Sound, Tacoma, Washington, USA.

He also served for 15 years as a town councillor in Baden-Württemberg in the south of Germany and was thus keenly interested in questions of local democracy, where the Nordic countries offer a sharp contrast to the Scottish situation.

When he once explained the Scottish system of local governance to a Finnish colleague, he nearly fell off his char in disbelief. While Scotland has 1,223 elected councillors covering the whole of Scotland in 32 'local' councils, Finland has 311 councils with over 10,000 elected councillors.

As a committed 'folkie', Paddy published four volumes on Hamish Henderson, the 'father of the Scottish folk revival' – and there is another yet to be published. He also published books and articles in learned journals on Irish and Scottish politics, society and culture and on UK devolution and European regionalism.

Paddy died suddenly in Edinburgh in February 2017 while completing this book. We miss him hugely.

IN NOVEMBER 1994, when Sweden voted in a referendum to join the European Union, it marked the culmination of four years of negotiations. 52.3 per cent of those who voted – the turnout was an impressive 83 per cent – voted in favour, and Sweden joined in 1995, alongside Finland and Austria.

The decision was not without controversy, to put it mildly. Opponents, particularly among the Greens and parts of the Social Democratic Party, questioned the neoliberal direction the EU was apparently adopting, criticised the loss of sovereignty and highlighted threats to the cherished state of Swedish neutrality. Asked to list the issues that mattered most, the EU opponents put the welfare state only fourth. Their two biggest worries were about democracy and sovereignty; national control of interest rates came third. Per Gahrton, a Green Party member of the Swedish Parliament, commented on the day it ratified the referendum's outcome: 'This is the day that the Riksdag decided to transform Sweden from an independent nation to a sort of province within an expanding superpower, in the process converting itself from a legislative body to little more than an advisory panel.'

Promoters of EU membership, led by the Social Democrat Ingvar Carlsson and the Conservative leader Carl Bildt, championed Sweden in the EU because in their view, membership was the only way of avoiding economic decline and, consequently, a weakening of the welfare state. However, Tage Erlander – Prime Minister between 1946 and 1969 – insisted 'it would be a dreadful mistake to allow economic factors to determine Swedish foreign policy.' For him, it was clear: 'We will co-operate with Europe, but Sweden's neutrality prevents us from seeking full membership.'

But now that the Cold War had ended, Ingvar Carlsson dismissed arguments about independence and sovereignty: 'National politicians have a formal decision-making power,' he declared just before the vote, 'over an increasing powerlessness.' Instead, Sweden could make a positive contribution to the shaping of EU policy, to develop it in a social-democratic direction.

In the previous two decades, the pressure for joining the EU had come mainly from the Conservatives. But after the Single Market was launched in 1993, fear grew about being frozen out.

In 1990, Carlsson still maintained that, 'in order for Sweden to become a member of the EEC, one of two conditions would have to be met: Either we must be assured that the risk of war in Europe has been completely eliminated; or, the EEC must decide not to develop a common defence and foreign policy.'

So news that the Swedish government was seeking EU membership later that same year came as a surprise, even a shock – not just for many Swedes, but also for neighbouring Finland. The Finns were clearly miffed that they had not been consulted on that dramatic policy change. Opponents were also concerned at the perceived bias of the media – in favour of EU membership, and the infinitely greater resources enjoyed by the 'yes' campaign, compared to those available to the 'no' camp.

The finale was frantic. With the Social Democrats' election victory in September 1994, the 'yes' side received perhaps the decisive boost, while the 'no' side had to grapple with a huge diversity within its ranks. The dominant force advocating a 'no' vote were groups on the left, environmentalist groups, and activists defending the 'Swedish model' of a progressive welfare state. But the 'no' side also comprised anti-immigrant and racist groups on the far right, many of whom were associated with the Sweden Democrats, a nationalist-populist far-right party rooted in white supremacist and Nazi ideology.

Thus, the main arguments hinged on sovereignty and the

loss of democracy versus the promise of prosperity, higher levels of employment and a boost for the Swedish welfare state. Among the most reluctant groups in society were low-paid Swedish women, many of whom were won around by the last-minute appeals of Lillemor Arvidsson, the popular leader of the female-dominated union of municipal workers, and by the deputy prime minister, Mona Sahlin. Also, Finance Minister Göran Persson's threat of heavy cuts in social benefits seemed to have persuaded many reluctant women voters to back the EU proposal.

In the end, the 52:48 acceptance of the proposed EU membership was regarded by observers and commentators as surprisingly comfortable. A closer look at the voting patterns revealed that 'yes' was supported far more by men than by women, that white-collar workers were more positively disposed towards the EU than industrial workers, and that the EU had more friends among the old than the young. City-dwellers voted overwhelmingly for EU membership while, as in Finland and Norway, rural areas were much more sceptical.

The result of the Swedish referendum was warmly welcomed by the EU and its member states. And that was not just because Sweden would be a net contributor to the EU coffers, but because Sweden was viewed favourably by most Europeans. A 1993 opinion survey among EU citizens had shown that Sweden was the most desirable of all potential new member-states. That was mainly because Sweden was perceived as a leader in social and environmental policies, and also as a seasoned advocate of peace, bringing a considerable amount of soft power to the EU. Jacques Delors, who retired as the EU's Commission President in January 1995, saw Sweden's accession as the fulfillment of his vision:

Now I can leave my post with full confidence in the future. Sweden will make a great contribution. I believe that the Nordic model of society will have an impact and change the EU's social and economic policies in a direction that appeals to me, personally.

In reality, post-Delors EU was not exactly heading for the social democratic dreamland, but rather embraced neo- and ordo-liberal ideologies. Despite that, a Swedish opinion poll held on the 20th anniversary of the referendum produced a 57:23 ratio affirming that the decision in 1994 had been the right one. The Swedish population has risen by nearly ten per cent in those two decades. The Swedish economy has done pretty well – GDP per capita now standing at around $50,000, double what it was just before joining the EU. Nearly 60 per cent of Sweden's trade is with other EU member states. And it could be even higher were it not for the fact that Norway, one of Sweden's main trading partners, decided to remain outside the European Union.

But polls in the late 1990s and early 2000s started to show a different picture: as Euroscepticism started to sweep through Europe. So, when it came to making a decision on joining the euro, the Swedes voted to stay outside the common currency, in a referendum on 14 September 2003, by a margin of 56 per cent to 42. The yes campaign had tried to counter concerns about loss of sovereignty with arguments about increasing influence. The leaders of all the biggest parties and of most of Sweden's largest companies argued that the country risked being marginalised in the EU if it shunned the euro. As in 1994, such arguments resonated with diplomats, international businessmen and the wealthy (Stockholm's richest suburb voted 75 per cent in favour) but did not overly-impress ordinary voters.

The yes campaigners tried, above all, to focus the debate on the economy. But, as exit polls showed, economic issues mattered less than expected. When Sweden voted to join the EU in 1994, its economy was in big trouble. But in 2003, Sweden enjoyed a growth rate of 1.5 per cent (against 0.5 per cent for the euro zone); Swedish unemployment stood at 5.4 per cent (against 8.9 per cent in the euro-countries). But the same exit polls that accurately predicted the euro referendum outcome also showed that 60 per cent of voters still favoured basic EU membership.

In a tragic development that would find an echo in the UK Brexit campaign, Anna Lindh, the country's popular and charismatic foreign minister, was stabbed to death in a Stockholm department store just three days before the poll. She had been one of the euro-campaigners' most prominent standard-bearers, and many expected a late surge of sympathy in favour of a yes. And, indeed, for the first time in months, a couple of opinion polls in the aftermath of the murder showed the yes camp ahead or level. But again like the English Brexit vote after the murder of Labour MP Jo Cox in her constituency, the Swedes were not emotionally swayed. They decided to keep their krona.

After the financial crash of 2008, the Swedish economy also took a hit. Exacerbated by the fact that a Conservative alliance under prime minister Fredrik Reinfeldt had come into office, the Swedish model came under immense pressure. By the time a Social Democrat re-gained power in 2014, over 16bn euro had been cut from taxes, largely at the expense of welfare. Unemployment had risen to over eight per cent. Moreover, according to the OECD, income inequality had grown faster in Sweden in the preceding 25 years than in any other industrialised nation. Growing youth unemployment, growing inequality and weakened welfare provision aided by a dollop of police insensitivity led to the anti-immigration riots of 2014.

Sweden, a nation of net emigration up to the First World

War, had become an immigrant nation by the end of the Second World War. Since the early 1970s, immigration to Sweden has been mostly due to the influx of refugees. In recent years, the number of people coming to Sweden seeking asylum has increased markedly. In 2014, the number of asylum applications rose to over 80,000, an increase of 50 per cent over the previous year.

Sweden's liberal immigration regime means that roughly 15 per cent of the population (9.5m) was born abroad and that 27 per cent of the Swedish population is of at least partly foreign descent. A minority of both first and second generation immigrants have found integrating difficult and complain of discrimination.

But those riots did not signal the breakdown of the social compact in Sweden. The Swedish model is not broken. The riots were a challenge, particularly in the working-class suburbs of the cities, where immigrant communities make up to around 80 per cent of the local population. There, in the concrete jungle of these sub/urban areas, like Husby, trust in governance and hope for the future are thinly spread. While upward mobile immigrants move into 'Swedish' neighbourhoods, sending their kids to good schools, those new arrivals who do not speak the language and are not familiar with Swedish culture often move into those quarters which already have a surfeit of problems. While in inner-city Stockholm 97 per cent of primary school kids have good grades in all subjects, in Hjulsta the figure is below 30 per cent. Every fifth 15-year-old in Husby does not attend school at all. Four out of ten 20-year-olds do not have a job or an apprenticeship.

The Social Democrats came back to power in 2014 because many Swedes decided their country had gone down the wrong route and was becoming too unequal. Initially, the tax-cutting regime had been welcomed. Public coffers were, over the two parliamentary periods of Reinfeldt, relieved of 140 bn krona annually (15bn euro), private households got richer. But in a very unequal fashion. While the better-off in their villas could easily increase their accounts by up to €4,000 a year, the low-wage earners like nurses in their rented accommodation could perhaps hope to be €200 better off at the end of the year.

While Sweden was, in 1996, world-wide the most equal society, by 2014 it had slid down the table to 14th in terms of income and wealth distribution. No other OECD country saw a greater widening of the gap between rich and poor than Sweden since 2007. And in no other country was the level of aid for the sick and unemployed cut as massively as in Reinfeldt's Sweden. Public infrastructure began to show stress symptoms: waiting times in hospitals lengthened, schools complained about lacking sufficient resources, and social care suffered from under-funding and staff shortages. Lower tax revenues tore holes into the welfare net.

Swedes, like everyone else, like tax cuts – but not necessarily when they undermine the welfare system. The cultural editor of *Aftonbladet* explained: 'Swedes are a social democratic people and they want social democratic policies. They are proud of their social system and expect that it is there for them, and for everyone else as well.'

Reinfeldt had promised to improve welfare on lower taxes – but he could not deliver. Stefan Löfven, elected prime minister in 2014, campaigned on substantial investments into that welfare system, investment into neglected infrastructure and the creation of new jobs, backed by tax rises of €10bn.

Worryingly, the far-right Sweden Democrats won 49 seats in the 2014 election and became, with a 12.9 per cent share of the vote, the third-strongest party in the Riksdag. Technically, they are holding the balance of power – but none of the other parties want to work with them. Their anti-immigration stance (they want to reduce it by 90 per cent) as well as their demand for a referendum on Sweden's EU membership (advocating a Swexit) have isolated them in the Riksdag.

But, only a couple of months after the election, the Sweden Democrats nearly succeeded in bringing the Red-Green minority government of Löfven down by voting down the budget and backing the alternative proposal of the centre-right parties. It took negotiations down to the wire before the government could secure the support of this and future budgets through an agreement with the Alliance parties, at the price of concessions regarding immigration policy, defence and pensions.

The acute refugee crisis of 2015 and 2016 put intense pressure on Europe's passport-free Schengen zone, in which Sweden is a member. At the beginning of 2016, Sweden re-imposed controls on visitors crossing from Denmark across what had been one of the most open borders in the world. Only hours after the measures came into effect, Denmark announced it would introduce new controls on its own border with Germany, while Berlin warned the 26-nation zone of passport-free travel was now 'in danger'.

Sweden's new controls represented a turnaround for the Nordic nation which, by that time, had taken in more asylum seekers per capita than any other European country. Although the left-of-centre government had initially welcomed the Syrian, Iraqi and Afghan refugees who swept across Europe since mid-2015, it only expected about 100,000 to make it to Sweden, many of them through Denmark. The final figure for 2015 was more than 160,000, which put a strain on essential local services. These new controls did not just reverse the Schengen agreement, signed in 1985 and implemented in 1995 (signed by Sweden in 1996 and implemented in 2001), but was also a setback to the post-1945 Nordic Council tradition of open borders that includes the five-nation Nordic Passport Union, which came into force in 1957.

Around the time of the UK referendum on EU membership there was a lot of speculation – and hope among the hardline Brexiteers – that a Brexit victory in the UK could pave the way for Sweden to leave the EU as well – Swexit, as it were. Some feared – or hoped – for a 'domino effect' – Denmark, Sweden, Holland, France, even Austria, were lined up as the most likely countries to follow the UK example. Doubtless, Nigel Farage salivated at the prospect of a break-up of the European Union itself. But, a series of opinion polls in those countries showed that the Brexit victory had the opposite effect. The approval rate of the EU rose, and demands for EU referenda declined.

While a poll before the UK vote suggested that only 32 per cent of Swedes would want to remain in the EU if the UK left, with 36 per cent in favour of a so-called Swexit, polls after the Brexit decision saw the remain position in Sweden soar to over 60 per cent. The situation in Denmark was broadly similar. Public confidence in the EU surged in the month after the UK referendum from 38 to 48 per cent, according to a Novus poll.

Although the Swedes have become more enthusiastic about the country's EU membership over the last 15 years, there have been downsides. One downside has been a process of wage dumping. It has become much easier to undermine the Swedish employment model – which was very highly regulated and had very good wages – by using foreign labour. The Swedes have tried to adapt to that and compensate for it. But there are other areas of the economy where they have had to take away protection and controls that were quite critical to the way Swedish society was run since the Second World War.

What most Swedes understand is that life in the EU is a trade-off. No country is ever completely sovereign; it is always in a process of negotiation. The understanding that EU membership is a matter of give and take is shared amongst all the Nordic countries. It is important to emphasise that being in the EU is not a Utopian dream, and sometimes – as seen from a current Swedish perspective – not even a universally good thing. But that does not mean Sweden is about to follow the UK – which it always regarded as a very close partner – out of the Union.

What could be important for Scotland, from a Swedish perspective, is the way the Swedes have used the EU as a foreign policy tool. It's part of the same outlook that means the Swedes have used the UN far more than some other countries. Sweden has discovered that the European Union, and particularly the European Parliament, offers a very good platform for pushing some of its softer aims in terms of environmental protection and human rights. They are very proactive within the EU along those lines, not trying to control things, but pushing them in the right direction, often with an immense amount of frustration when they face colleagues from the more reactionary Eastern European parties.

But despite these difficulties, Swedish people believe they have gained from being a small country in the EU – a Nordic nation at the crossroads of many different worlds.

8

Finland – Totally in and helping to write the EU rulebook

TUOMAS ISO-MARKKU

FINLAND

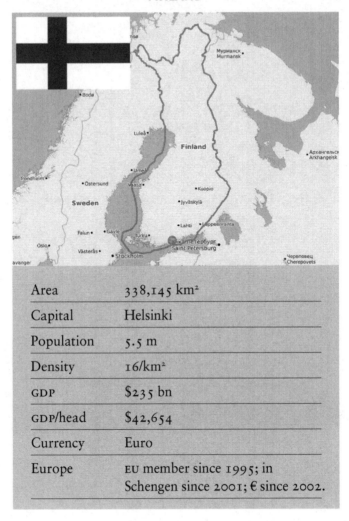

Area	338,145 km²
Capital	Helsinki
Population	5.5 m
Density	16/km²
GDP	$235 bn
GDP/head	$42,654
Currency	Euro
Europe	EU member since 1995; in Schengen since 2001; € since 2002.

MCSMÖRGÅSBORD: SCOTLAND AND THE NORDICS

TUOMAS ISO-MARKKU speaks fluent Finnish, Spanish and German, very good English, pretty good Swedish and a bit of Polish. But that is not totally unusual for a Finn. As Tuomas says:

Let's face it. Being Finnish means you must learn another language fast. With Finnish alone you are getting nowhere. My first foreign language was German, which I started learning at the age of nine. Then English aged 11, and Swedish at 13. I learned Spanish at university in my 20s. I'm now fluent because I have a brilliant teacher – my Spanish-born girlfriend. But I wish my Swedish was better. I have paid less attention to it – not because of language policy reasons (Swedish is Finland's second official language because Sweden ruled Finland until 1809, but nationalistic forces have recently questioned the status of the Swedish language in Finnish society) but simply because I lived in Berlin for almost eight years.

Actually, I want Finland to remain an officially bi-lingual country even though most Finnish-speaking Finns are like me and don't

speak much Swedish. I like the idea of a multi-lingual society and
think that having (at least) two languages is part of Finland's cultural
tradition. It also connects us more firmly to our Nordic neighbours.

That desire for connection with western neighbours is typical of
the folk who inhabit the remotest region in the European Union
and live cheek by jowl with Russia. If Scotland is in bed with an
elephant – as Ludovic Kennedy once described the Caledonian
relationship with England – the Finns are in bed with a bear. No
wonder they have become the world's most sensitive
negotiators, with former PM Martti Ahtisaari picking up the
Nobel Peace Prize in 2008.

Tuomas was born in Helsinki, but his family moved 120 km
west to Salo when he was just a few weeks old. Salo had a
population of slightly over 20,000 back then, but in the 1990s
the town grew rapidly, attracting a workforce from all over
Finland and even abroad. The boom had to do with the Finnish
mobile phone giant Nokia. One of Nokia's biggest factories,
along with a sizeable production development unit, was
situated in Salo, and a huge proportion of the population
worked for Nokia or its suppliers, earning Salo the nickname
'the Silicon Valley of Finland'. But Nokia's troubles on the
mobile phone market led to massive layoffs in 2009 and finally
to the closure of the factory in 2012. In 2014 Nokia was bought
by Microsoft, which struck the next blow against Salo, closing
the production development unit and laying off all the
remaining 1,100 employees. So Salo has gone from being a
sleepy provincial town to the hub of the digital revolution and
back again. Salo's experience illustrates Finland's
transformation from a rural society into an advanced industrial
and technological player with the highest level of R&D
spending in the EU – but it also reflects the country's recent
economic woes.

Tuomas's approach to the near total shutdown of his hometown is typically philosophical: 'The big mistakes were made long before the Microsoft takeover.'

In his early life, Tuomas had a typically Finnish upbringing. His parents still have a summer house which they bought when he was 17. It is not far away – in fact it is just ten minutes away in the next village. But it is next to a lake – and that is very important. 'At week-ends we drive there, heat the sauna and go for a swim. Afterwards we stay drinking beer or having a barbecue.' It sounds idyllic, but it is the Finnish norm.

So too is military service – in fact, it is obligatory. The 19-year-old Tuomas was lucky to be posted on a picturesque island in the Finnish Archipelago Sea observing maritime traffic. It was a fairly informal atmosphere with plenty of spare time which let him study for the entrance exam to Turku University where he studied European Contemporary history.

During that degree, the European Union unknowingly made a big change to his life. Tuomas could spend one year in an EU member state through the EU-funded Erasmus programme, so he opted for Germany on the basis that German was his first foreign language and would be more difficult to learn without immersion. In Bochum, an industrial city in the Ruhr valley (and, coincidentally, the site of another large Nokia factory), he met his Spanish-born girlfriend – also an EU exchange student. After finishing his Bachelor's degree in Turku, Tuomas and his girlfriend moved to Berlin. While living in Berlin, Tuomas commuted to the small town of Frankfurt an der Oder at the German-Polish border, where he completed a German-Polish dual degree in European studies and political science.

Some classes took place at the Collegium Polonicum, an institute run jointly by the University in Frankfurt an der Oder and the Adam Mickiewicz University in Poznan. During his studies,

Tuomas experienced Poland's accession to the Schengen zone, which made a massive difference to students. All of a sudden, they no longer needed to show passports to attend classes on the other side of the border. It was quite a concrete demonstration of how the EU can change things.

Both Tuomas and his girlfriend enjoyed living in Berlin, so the couple stayed there for almost eight years until a job came up in Helsinki and they moved north. Was that a good move?

> Helsinki is very different from Berlin which is a really buzzing cultural hub. Helsinki is a very relaxed place and we can go everywhere by bike or walk – it doesn't take 45 minutes to get somewhere. My girlfriend grew up by the Atlantic Ocean so she is beside the sea again. We can see it from our window.

And is political life in Finland as peaceful?

> It has always been important for Finland to establish a reputation as a constructive and pragmatic actor in Europe – always ready to reach agreement. Many are afraid that reputation has been lost because of Finland's actions in recent years. The previous government took a very tough position in the negotiations about the bailouts for the crisis-ridden euro countries and the current government abstained from voting on the EU's refugee relocation scheme. This has had an impact on how other countries see Finland. Internally, Finland, like so many other European countries, has experienced a growing political polarization, which is a worrying trend. Luckily, Finland has well-working and stable democratic institutions.

Right now, Tuomas is working as a Research Fellow at the Finnish Institute of International Affairs, where he deals with a number of topics, including the EU's Common Security and Defence Policy, Finnish EU policy, German EU policy, the European Parliament and, most recently, Euroscepticism and populism.

IN THE FOLLOWING, I will argue that Finland is the most EU-minded of the Nordic countries. This might sound surprising, considering that one of the topics foreign journalists and researchers have most often asked me about in recent years has been Finnish Euroscepticism. The strong interest in Finnish Euroscepticism is related to the rapid rise of the Eurosceptic and populist Finns Party (formerly known as True Finns), which was very successful in the Finnish parliamentary elections in 2011 and 2015 and currently forms part of the Finnish government coalition. However, while it is true that Finland's relationship with the EU has become more complicated in recent years, compared to its Nordic peers, Finland remains a very 'European' country.

So, why is Finland different from the other Nordic countries in terms of its relationship with the EU? There are three aspects to this question which I will try to address. First, I want to briefly describe in what ways and to what extent Finland actually differs from the other Nordic countries when it comes to its relationship with the EU. And I will argue that Finland is indeed the most 'European' country among them, the country most integrated into the EU. Then I will try and explain the reasons for that. Finally, I will look into the changes that have occurred in recent years, asking whether Finland will continue to be the most integrated and EU-minded Nordic state.

Starting with a short historical overview, Denmark, Norway and Sweden were among the founding members of the European Free Trade Association (EFTA), which was established in 1959. As for Finland, the country had to balance its relations with Western institutions. This was because of its difficult relationship with the Soviet Union, rooted in the two wars the countries fought between 1939 and 1944. In 1948, Finland and the Soviet Union concluded the Treaty on Friendship, Cooperation and Mutual

Assistance, which largely determined the basic objectives of Finnish foreign and security policy for the whole of the Cold War period: maintaining friendly relations with the Soviet Union and pursuing a policy of neutrality to avoid involvement in the conflicts of the great powers.

Despite its challenging international position, Finland signed an association agreement with EFTA in 1961. An important factor behind the integration policies of all the Nordic states at that time was the UK, whose market was of great importance for all of them, especially for Denmark, Norway, Sweden and Finland. Consequently, these Nordic countries closely followed what was happening in the UK and what kind of trade arrangements the UK was seeking. The UK's decision to join the European Communities (EC) in 1973 was the reason why Denmark chose to become a member, too, and the reason why Finland, Iceland, Norway and Sweden all signed free trade agreements with the European Economic Community (EEC) around the same time.

The free trade agreement with the EEC prompted a very heated debate in Finland because of Finland's special relationship with the Soviet Union. At the same time as Finland signed the free trade agreement with the EEC, different arrangements were developed to remove trade barriers with the Soviet Union and several countries of the Council for Mutual Economic Assistance (COMECON).

The treaty with the EEC was, in the end, as far as Finland was ready to go during the Cold War period. Finland did join EFTA as a full member in 1986, long after the initial Association Agreement. However, until the end of the Cold War, Finland and Sweden were strictly neutral states whose participation in the European integration process was very limited.

In this context, it may be interesting to shed some light on the relations between the Nordic countries and NATO.

Denmark, Norway and Iceland were among the founding members of NATO. But Finland and Sweden, due to their neutral status in the Cold War period, did not even consider NATO membership. And even after the end of the Cold War, Finland and Sweden have remained outside NATO, even though they no longer define themselves as neutral countries, instead talking about being militarily non-allied. In the Finnish case, the most recent formulation is simply 'Finland is not a member of a military alliance'. But in both Finland and Sweden there has been occasionally heated debate about the possibility of joining NATO at some future point.

But back to the EU. Denmark has been a member since 1973; Finland and Sweden joined in 1995, and Norway rejected the possibility of joining the EU in two referenda, with the latter taking place right after the Finnish and Swedish membership referenda. Denmark, despite being the longest-serving Nordic EU member state, has opt-outs related to several areas of EU policy, like the economic and monetary union (not being part of the Eurozone) and also regarding defence policy, justice and home affairs, and EU citizenship issues.

Sweden, similarly, rejected participation in the Eurozone in a separate referendum in 2003. That makes Finland the only Nordic EU member state inside the Eurozone. Finland was among the first countries to join the common currency.

If we ask what made Finland choose the EU, and also what made it take a more favourable position on integration than the other Nordic member states, here are some of the basic reasons:

As far as the factors that led Finland to apply for EU membership are concerned, the first one was actually Sweden's somewhat unexpected decision to apply in 1991. I know there is still a trauma among the Finnish politicians of that time because Sweden announced its intention to apply for EU membership without consulting Finland first. So the Swedish decision came as a big surprise to Finnish decision-makers and had a huge impact on the debate in Finland. But Sweden's decision was what actually started the debate in Finland about joining the EU.

In the 1990s, Finland was dealing with a heavy recession that was partly exacerbated by the fact that Finland's substantial trade relations with the Soviet Union had, more or less, collapsed. Thus, the membership debate was very much driven by economic concerns, too.

Another big issue was the idea that Finland should be able to exert influence on the policies that affected it. Finland was actually negotiating the possibility of joining the European Economic Area (EEA) – an alternative to EU membership – almost at the same time as negotiating its membership in the EU. Eventually, Finland joined the EEA in 1994, only one year before it joined the EU. And one thing that made EU membership more attractive to Finland was simply the fact that, as an EU member, Finland could be there at the table when decisions concerning the single market were taken, whereas, as an EEA member, Finland would have been left outside the decision-making process.

Then there were the security policy considerations. Just when Finland was discussing the possibility of joining the EU, the moribund Soviet Union, and later Russia, were going through a period of great instability. Under these conditions, the EU was seen in Finland, almost from the very beginning, as a potential stabilising force, even though the Union did not have a very extensive foreign or security policy remit at the time.

Despite the lack of an EU security and defence policy, it was bluntly stated that the EU would help Finland protect itself from any threats, be they of military or political nature.

That became a very big factor, especially in the latter part of the Finnish EU debate. At first, the debate was more about economic concerns and about Finland being more influential within the EU than outside of it. But security policy concerns became very important as the Finnish EU debate evolved.

Finally, there were what one might call 'identity issues'. There was a sense that EU membership would confirm and strengthen, Finland's Western, or European, identity. This had, at least from the Finnish point of view, been questioned during the Cold War because of Finland's somewhat unclear position between the power blocs.

There were of course also several arguments against EU membership in Finland, and some of them were simply the mirror image of the arguments used in favour of EU membership. Thus, instead of gaining influence, it was argued that Finland as a small state might end up losing influence by joining the EU, where it might not have any say at all. From the very beginning, there was also the argument that EU membership would be incompatible with neutrality, which had been such an important concept for Finland during the Cold War period. But that was overcome by re-interpreting Finland's status from a stance of full-scale neutrality to one of military non-alliance, which did not exclude the possibility of joining a political union. Another substantial concern was related to the future of the Finnish agricultural sector. Finally, there were also fears that EU membership might endanger Finland's relatively high levels of social, political and gender equality.

But, notwithstanding these arguments (and reflecting voting patterns in other EU states), EU membership was favoured almost universally among Finland's political and economic elites. However, the general public, and therefore also Finland's political parties, were more divided.

Nevertheless, all of Finland's three major parties – the Centre Party, the National Coalition Party and the Social Democratic Party – officially favoured EU membership, even though the grand majority of the Centre Party voters were against it. The rather small Swedish People's Party also backed membership.

Two Finnish parties – the Left Party and the Green Party – were so divided among themselves that they chose not to adopt any official position on the membership question. That left two parties, which were clearly against EU membership: the Christian Democratic Party and the Finnish Rural Party which was the predecessor of the Finns Party, the Eurosceptic party of today.

So the political and economic elites were mostly or almost universally in favour of EU membership. But one group was almost universally against EU membership: the Finnish farmers. More than 90 per cent of them voted against EU membership in the EU referendum.

The EU referendum produced a result of 56.9 per cent in favour of membership and 43.1 per cent against. That might not look like a massive majority, but it meant that Finland's membership was endorsed by a bigger majority than in Sweden.

There was a clear centre/periphery divide in the vote. The urban areas of Finland were much more favourable towards membership than peripheral and rural regions, most of which voted against. There was one exception, though: in the rural south-eastern part of Finland, which is relatively sparsely populated and right next to the border with Russia, a clear majority voted in favour of EU membership. This might have to do with the idea of EU membership as some sort of security guarantee.

Turning to the question of why Finland, once inside the EU, took a strong pro-integration view, I would say a crucial aspect was that the divisions the EU referendum had caused were overcome astonishingly quickly – largely thanks to Finland's very consensual political culture.

Immediately after Finland joined the EU in 1995, there were elections and after them a very broad government coalition was established. It was called the Rainbow Coalition, because it included parties from across the political spectrum, from the Left Party, which had not adopted an official position on the EU question at all, to the centre-right National Coalition Party and the Swedish People's Party, both of which had been very enthusiastic about the possibility of EU membership. As part of this big coalition government, even the Left Alliance and the Green League adopted a very positive approach to the EU, subscribing to the Government's view that Finland should be as close to the core of the EU as possible.

Finland's pro-integration stance was also related to Finland wanting to be an influential player within the EU. It was felt that if Finland is in the EU, it must be at all tables where important decisions were being made. This, on the other hand, required being fully involved in the major areas of EU integration. That was clearly a major factor when Finland chose to participate in the Eurozone. Unlike in Denmark and Sweden, there was no referendum on the Euro. The Finnish Government took the view that Finland had already accepted the idea of joining the Euro in its accession agreement, and that therefore a referendum was not necessary. It may also have to do with the fact the Finland does not really have a tradition of referenda. We have only had two in the history of independent Finland – one on the abolition of Prohibition, and the second on the EU membership. We only vote on very important matters.

The Finnish Parliament decided on Euro membership and it was quite a divisive issue. For example, the opposition parties voted against it, and the population was also quite divided. It is hard to say how a referendum would have turned out, but I recently read that the polls just before the parliamentary decision indicated that 47 per cent would have been in favour and 41 per cent against. Thus, a referendum might have led to the same result, that is, to Finland joining the Eurozone.

All in all, Finland quickly became a pro-integration, pro-European country because a very broad EU policy consensus emerged. And even though the parties in the governing coalition shifted after the Rainbow Coalition was voted out of government, their EU policies did not shift in any very dramatic way. Indeed, there was the idea that Finland – and this is partly related to the political consensus – should present a unified stance when in Brussels, because only in this way would Finland actually be able to influence decisions there.

And then there is Finland's self-perception as a small member state. It may sound a bit funny, compared to, say, the Faroe Islands, that we cultivate this strong small state identity, but it is in fact a major part of Finland's political DNA. There was an implicit understanding that Finland as a small member state should always be a constructive player within the EU. It would be better not to make too much noise, and rather be part of the solution than be part of the problem.

There was also the belief that, as a small member state, Finland would be best protected if there were strong rules and institutions. This led Finland to be a strong supporter of the European Commission, for example, and of the so-called 'community method', which emphasises the role of EU's community institutions such as the Commission and the European Parliament.

A further reason for Finland's positive attitude towards

integration was the importance that the country attached to the EU in terms of security. Very soon after joining the EU, Finland defined the basic elements of its security and defence policy as consisting of military non-alliance, independent defence and EU membership.

It is also noteworthy that in the early membership period, there was no explicitly Eurosceptic party in the Finnish Parliament. Eurosceptic ideas were mainly represented by individual members of Finland's established political parties. These came especially from the Left Party and from the Centre Party, both of which had had difficulties in positioning themselves in the membership question. However, Eurosceptic ideas did not have much relevance, as EU issues were generally at the margins of the political debate and were not deemed as very important by the parties or the general public.

Public support for the EU may have not been very high in Finland at any point during the country's membership period but, at the same time, there has constantly been a very high percentage of citizens who hold a neutral position on the EU. In most cases, I would argue that these citizens can be classified as latent supporters of the EU. If Finland's membership in the EU were to be questioned, these people would most likely say 'no, we want to stay in'.

What has changed in Finland's relationship in the EU in the last few years? Since the outbreak of the Eurozone crisis, EU issues have become much more politicised and contested in Finland. To some extent, this has to do with the pro-integrationist policy consensus, which long characterised Finnish EU policy. In the latter part of the 2000s, many voters started to take the view that the positions of the main parties had become too similar on several issues, including EU policy. That helped the Eurosceptic Finns Party – previously known as True Finns – a lot, allowing the party to position itself as credible challenger of the established political parties.

The Eurozone crisis, and the bailouts, which proved hugely unpopular in Finland, have also had a substantial effect. The Finns Party turned the bailouts into a major campaign topic in the Finnish parliamentary elections in 2011, cultivating the narrative that Finland had taken very good care of its economy, whereas some of the southern EU member states had not and arguing that Finland should not assume responsibility for their problems. The strategy proved effective, helping the Finns Party to almost quintuple its vote share (from 4.1 per cent to 19.1 per cent) and become Finland's third-biggest parliamentary party. The success of the Finns Party made the other Finnish parties more cautious about the EU, especially on issues related to the Eurozone and economic solidarity between the member states.

But I would argue that the factors which made Finland initially more EU-minded than the rest of the Nordic states still pertain. There is still a very consensual political culture. The Finns Party is currently part of the government coalition, and in order to join the government it had to moderate its positions quite a lot and subscribe to a largely pro-European government programme, which emphasises the importance of deepening the Single Market and enhancing the Common Security and Defence Policy. As part of the government coalition, the Finns Party was also forced to accept a further bailout package for Greece, an idea it vehemently opposed. All this has had a negative impact on the party's popularity. Its polling results in the past year have been very bad, with the party falling below the ten per cent-mark.

It is also important to note that despite the controversial debates related to the bailouts, the basic rationale behind

Finnish EU membership has not changed dramatically since Finland joined the EU. Finland's membership is still about the economy and security, and this latter aspect has been highlighted by the Ukraine crisis, the ensuing tensions between the EU and Russia, and the military activity in the broader Baltic Sea region.

Finally, there have been no dramatic changes in the level of public support for the EU. All in all, Finland may thus have become a bit more cautious in its approach towards the EU, but membership in the Union is still very important for Finland and there are several areas of EU policy where Finland would like to see substantial progress, such as the single market and the Common Security and Defence Policy.

Let me link the discussion about Finland and its relationship with the EU to the situation in the UK and in Scotland after the Brexit decision. Brexit is not only a challenge for Scotland, and for the UK as a whole. It is also a big challenge for the EU and, I would argue, for every member state that is interested in the future of the EU. For Finland it also means losing an ally in some EU policy questions. Finland and the UK have shared very similar views regarding, amongst others, questions of trade policy.

But I think even more important from the Finnish point of view are the dynamics that the Brexit process has already set in motion and what they mean for the EU as a whole. What kind of an EU will there be in the future? And what is Finland's place in that EU going to look like?

Scotland's case is of course particularly interesting. The situation that Scotland now finds itself in shares some similarities with the situation in which Finland was in after the Cold War. Back then, the basic pillars which Finland's foreign, security and integration policy had been built on were all moving. And, in the Finnish case, that led to the

8

response that Finland wanted to join the EU and wanted to become a core member state within the EU. We will see what is going to happen in the Scottish case.

9

Options for Scotland

LESLEY RIDDOCH

9

SCOTLAND

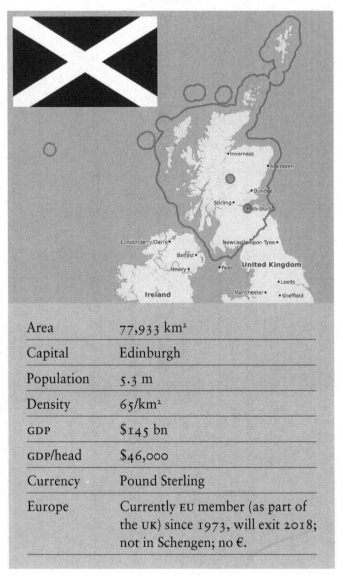

Area	77,933 km²
Capital	Edinburgh
Population	5.3 m
Density	65/km²
GDP	$145 bn
GDP/head	$46,000
Currency	Pound Sterling
Europe	Currently EU member (as part of the UK) since 1973, will exit 2018; not in Schengen; no €.

WHAT CONNECTED A Wolverhampton-born, Belfast-bred lass from a Scottish highland family with the Nordic nations?

Lesley Riddoch's mother came from Wick and her family – like many Caithnessians – were convinced they were Norse not Scots. Indeed, she had a grandfather, uncle and cousin all called Magnus More. But the most formative experience happened accidentally when she rented an abandoned cottage for seven glorious years in Glen Buchat, 45 minutes inland from Aberdeen.

> My 'bothy' was owned by a local farmer and had been occupied by
> a farm labourer and his family until the 1940s. It had a great roof
> but no electricity or running water. Without human occupation it

had become the domain of animals – it took years of weekend and summer stays to learn how to share that space with them. Cows wandered outside day and night – part of their cattle trough also served as my makeshift fridge.

I loved the freedom and the adventure. But I knew only a handful of people who felt the same. Until I went to Norway. Then my curiosity about the Nordic nations just grew and grew.

Lesley set up the policy group Nordic Horizons in 2010 with Dan Wynn and is one of Scotland's best known commentators and broadcasters. She was assistant editor of *The Scotsman* in the 1990s (and editor of *The Scotswoman* in 1995 when female staff wrote, edited and produced the paper) and contributing editor of the Sunday Herald. She is best known for broadcasting with programmes on BBC2, Channel 4, Radio 4 and BBC Radio Scotland, for which she has won two Sony speech broadcaster awards. Lesley runs her own independent radio and podcast company, Feisty Ltd which produces a popular weekly podcast and was a member of the three-year EU-funded Equimar marine energy project. Lesley is a weekly columnist for *The Scotsman* and *The National* and a regular contributor to *The Guardian, Scotland Tonight, Question Time* and *Any Questions*. She is also completing a PhD supervised by Oslo and Strathclyde Universities comparing the Scots and Norwegian hutting traditions. Lesley founded the charity *Africawoman* and the feminist magazine *Harpies and Quines* and was a member of the Isle of Eigg Trust, which led to the successful community buyout in 1997. She wrote *Riddoch on the Outer Hebrides* in 2007, *Blossom – what Scotland needs to Flourish* with Luath in 2013 and *Wee White Blossom – what post referendum Scotland needs to Flourish* in December 2014.

NO DOUBT SOME of the political speculation in this book will be out of date, the very day of publication – that's how fast events are moving thanks to Brexit, Trump and the prospect of Theresa May's Great Reform Bill and a second independence referendum. The political options for Scotland in Europe by comparison are relatively static and stable.

Firstly, Scotland could get a differentiated deal within the UK. No-one is holding their breath on that one. To date, the Prime Minister has not formally responded to the options paper handed in by the Scottish First Minister before Christmas 2016.

According to the Scottish external affairs Secretary Fiona Hyslop, Scotland's Place in Europe

> is not about trying to have a differentiated position as a separate independent country or indeed continuing EU membership. This is a compromise position and we expect the UK to move some way towards us, it can't be just one-way traffic.[1]

But the bottom line of a 'differentiated deal' would be that Scotland stays in the Single Market. Hyslop admits that is 'technically and legally challenging but… doable if there is a political will.'

It looks pretty clear now – there isn't.

So the second option is that an independent Scotland could choose to join EFTA and thus access the European Single Market via the EEA, and the third option is to remain inside the EU or immediately reapply for full membership.

As a wee reminder, the EEA is the mechanism that extends the EU's Single Market to the three participating states of EFTA – the European Free Trade Association. EFTA is an

---

1   Catriona Webster, 'Scotland's bid to remain in single market is "not dead"', *Edinburgh Evening News*, 19 January 2017.

alternative trading bloc to the EU formed in 1960 that has few institutions, very little wider social remit and no ambitions for further political integration. Iceland, Liechtenstein and Norway are EFTA members who are also in the EEA and thus have access to the EU's 500 million consumers – for a price.

Should an iScotland become EFTA/EEA state number four?

Of course, before anyone can consider the desirability of this 'halfway house' there's the inconvenient truth that Scotland is not currently independent and opinion polls are stuck (on average) at pre-Brexit levels – 47 per cent supporting independence and 53 per cent against.

But Scotland's vote to remain in the EU has highlighted more than different attitudes towards Europe, trade, immigration and integration north and south of the border. The high-handed manner of Brexit-related constitutional change and Theresa May's contemptuous rejection of attempts to achieve a Scottish opt-out have shone a deeply unflattering light on the UK's inflexibility towards smaller component member nations – an inflexibility that is fairly out of place in most of mainland Europe and pretty well non-existent in the Nordic Region.

Stubbornly insisting that no 'regional' deal for Scotland is possible (whilst preparing deals for East Anglian farmers, Nissan and the car industry, the City of London and in all probability Ireland and Gibraltar) Theresa May's 'my way or the highway' Britain contrasts visibly and unfavourably with 'you take the high road and I'll take the low road' permissive outlook of the Nordics.

The tiny Faroes (population 43,000) for example, already had such a powerful parliament in 1973 when 'Mother' Denmark chose to enter the EU that the Faroese Parliament simply voted not to join. When Greenland's parliament acquired enough powers, it too left the EU. Not easy – but evidently not impossible. Today Denmark backs the Faroes bid to join EFTA. No grudge matches there.

Within the Nordic Region, nations within larger states expect to be allowed to stick up for their own national interests without being regarded as selfish, errant children. Indeed they expect to have the power locally to take those big decisions themselves. The relaxed, consensual Nordic approach to constitutional change is very different from the defensive and confrontational argument in Britain. But it's taken the impending reality of Brexit to bring that into crystal clear focus.

Alex Salmond has pointed out that Liechtenstein and Switzerland are in a monetary union, a customs union, a passport union, but Liechtenstein, as an EFTA member, is in the European Economic Area, while fellow-EFTA member Switzerland is not. He called for 'political imagination' to give Scotland its own Brexit deal.[2] Jonathan Le Tocq, the former chief minister of Guernsey, now Guernsey's minister for external affairs, suggested that 'Scotland's best chances of securing a separate European deal was if the Scottish Parliament had a 'devo max' deal, where all powers are devolved, apart from defence and foreign affairs – the same arrangement as Guernsey, Jersey and the Isle of Man.'[3]

Indeed if Scotland was a constituent territory of Denmark or Norway not Britain, the case for a 'differentiated settlement' would probably have been accepted more readily and the constitutional changes needed to activate and support that different settlement would already be grinding their way through several parliaments.

---

2 Paris Gourtsoyannis, 'Liechtenstein viewed as blueprint as Salmond says Scottish deal is possible', *The Scotsman*, 30 January 2017.

3 Andrew Whitaker, 'Scotland could have 'devo max' deal in Europe', *Sunday Herald*, 5 February 2017.

Not here.

If Scotland is to remain inside the UK and remain within the EU or join EFTA (and thus remain in the EEA, the underlying single market mechanism), the Scottish Parliament would need the legal capacity to be able to sign international treaties – a power the tiny Faroe Islands have wielded since their truly powerful devolved parliament was established by Denmark in 1946.

Similarly, if Scotland is to preserve and develop the distinctive political culture that helped produce its hefty Remain majority, then more powers must logically come Holyrood's way. Firstly, powers currently exercised by Brussels but devolved to Scotland like agriculture and fisheries. Secondly, powers currently exercised by Brussels but reserved to Westminster, like workers' rights and health and safety. And, finally, powers like immigration which would be essential for a small nation navigating its way solo through the EU.

But none of that devolution looks certain or even likely.

Scotland's response to Britain's divided Brexit vote has been positively Nordic – Scots expect diversity and empowerment to be entirely possible. Westminster's reaction has been decidedly British.

One singer – one song. One deal for everyone – end of.

And even though Scots Secretary David Mundell has been adamant that 'whatever the circumstances, no devolved powers [returned to the UK after Brexit] will be re-reserved to Westminster', the Scottish Conservative leader Ruth Davidson thinks otherwise.[4]

Ms Davidson told a National Farmers Union Scotland conference in February 2017 it would be 'foolhardy' to give

---

4   Simon Johnson, 'Ruth Davidson: 'Foolhardy' to devolve all EU agriculture powers to Scotland after Brexit', *The Daily Telegraph*, 6 February 2017.

MSPs the power to create an entirely separate Scottish replacement for the EU's controversial Common Agricultural Policy after Brexit.

The Scottish Tory leader said she expected 'an almighty political row' over whether Westminster or Holyrood runs agriculture after powers are repatriated from Brussels.

She argued it would be wrong to create barriers within the UK domestic market – the destination of 85 per cent of Scotland's 'agri-exports' – by having different systems on both sides of the Border.

It looks as if, to quote Iain Macwhirter, 'Holyrood will have to fight every inch of the way to secure new powers, and guarantee old ones, when the post-Brexit Scotland bill comes before Westminster sometime after 2019.'[5]

All of this is relevant in considering which post-independence European path Scotland should take, because the chronic inflexibility and the impending economic, social and legal difficulties produced by Brexit may have hastened Scotland's moment of post-independence choice. But to make sure no knee-jerk decision is taken, Scots desperately need some distance from the shrill Brexit debate to decide which European destination is the right one. Former SNP leader Alex Salmond visited our Norwegian 'Euro Nordics' speaker Duncan Halley shortly after the October 2016 event, along with two other SNP MPs. Duncan spent several hours outlining the ecological advantages of joining EFTA and the EEA – principally controlling our own fish stocks again and deciding which land use to encourage through subsidy.

So might the Scottish Government 'do a Norway/Iceland' – aim at the EEA as the first step to full EU membership, but

---

5   Iain Macwhirter, 'Act of Union could be Brexit's first casualty', *Sunday Herald*, 11 February 2017.

show little disquiet if that halfway house becomes a permanent home? It's certainly possible.

Keeping inside the single market but outside the troublesome common fisheries and agriculture programmes (whilst ensuring an indy Scotland does not border a Brexited England with radically different customs arrangements) could be an attractive option.

Membership of EFTA could solve Scotland's trade problems, its Brexit problems as well as the Scottish fishermen's opposition to most things European.

For some a best-case scenario is that somehow Scotland joins EFTA before being part of a complete UK exit from the European Union

Robin McAlpine is Director of Common Weal:

> Admitting that on independence Scotland will be in EFTA and that we would then have to choose a route forward from there offers reassurance that Eurosceptics would still have some degree of agency on the EU issue if they vote for independence.[6]

But it's the freedom on key policy issues that makes the EFTA option seriously attractive. Being in EFTA means being in the single market but outside the customs union and EFTA members are completely free to agree their own trade deals with anyone outside the EU. So McAlpine thinks it is likely EFTA membership would also solve any trade difficulties between an independent Scotland and the rest-of-the-UK.

> There is a very straightforward solution to this and that's to agree a British Isles Trade Zone. The only way that there

---

6   Robin McAlpine, 'Why joining EFTA instead of the EU could be the answer for Scotland', CommonSpace, 2 February 2017, <www.commonspace.scot/articles/10240/robin- mcalpine-why-joining-efta-instead-eu-could-be-answer-scotland>.

would ever be tariffs on cross-border trade would be either if the UK insisted (and it exports more to us than we do to it so that would make no sense) or if Scotland was compelled. Scotland cannot be compelled to impose tariffs unless it is inside a customs union. Conveniently, EFTA is precisely inside the single market but outside the customs union. There is a fee to pay, but that fee gives all the rights of the single market (including free movement of people). But EFTA members are completely free to agree their own trade deals with anyone outside the EU.

In fact, EFTA already has 27 major international trade agreements and Scotland would inherit all of these upon membership.

So it's likely that EFTA would solve our rest-of-UK trade problem for us. And if it didn't, we'd be entirely free to negotiate a deal ourselves.

And of course, EFTA membership would mean being outside the Common Agricultural and Common Fisheries Policies, with potential advantages for Scotland.

Juxtaposing EU and EFTA membership, Robin McAlpine is adamant:

> EFTA solves problems the EU doesn't. The EU creates problems EFTA doesn't. EFTA imposes very few policies which harm Scottish interests while the EU does. EFTA won't campaign against Scottish independence while the EU (or some of its member states) will. And EFTA doesn't result in a political union with potential fascists while the EU certainly could.

These are the attractions of EFTA/EEA membership for an independent Scotland.

But what about the other option – full EU membership?

Political momentum is certainly steering us in that direction.

Much of the first independence referendum was played

out against the vexed issue of whether Scotland could stay within or swiftly rejoin the EU – but it was only the feasibility of the move that mattered, not its desirability. Back then senior European political figures suggested accession would be difficult or very slow. Now, the tune has changed.

Jacqueline Minor, the European Commission's head of representation in the UK, says Scotland would already be aligned with EU requirements and is therefore in a different starting position from any other countries applying for EU membership.

'I think, obviously, there are some things that would facilitate that process, namely that Scotland would at a previous point have been aligned with the European acquis.

So it would have a familiarity with European processes, it would probably still have on its statute books a fair amount of European rules, which would mean it was starting from a point different from other applicant countries, who normally have to go through the entire process of aligning their rules with European rules,' she said.

Previously Ms Minor had told at a Scottish Parliamentary Journalists' Association event that an iScotland would have to wait in line with other countries such as Montenegro, Serbia and Bosnia and Herzegovina to join the EU.

Meanwhile on Valentine's Day 2017, the EU's chief Brexit negotiator Guy Verhofstadt sent a 'lovebomb' message to Scotland – 'Europe hasn't forgotten that a large majority of the Scottish people voted to Remain. We need the Scottish people and their firm European beliefs. Scotland has shaped European civilisation, through iconic figures such as David Hume, Alexander Fleming and Adam Smith and still does so today by being at the forefront of defining and strengthening European values. We cannot afford to lose that.'

In 2016 the Irish Parliament openly backed Scotland's bid for renewed Single Market membership however it is obtained – from within or without the UK. England is Ireland's biggest market and closest neighbour and, two short years ago, Irish politicians calculated it would not be in their country's best interests to take on England over Scottish independence. Today, bets are off. Westminster's contemptuous and curmudgeonly attitude towards Europe appears to have sealed the deal between the Celts, and Nicola Sturgeon's cogent Brexit statement may yet seal the deal with European neighbours further afield. 'Attitudes to Scotland are almost totally inverted compared to 2014,' observed Alyn Smith MEP: 'We're the good guys now, not the awkward squad.'[7]

So the once frosty European Union is warming to the prospects of Scottish independence because it means one small new member might arrive just as a large old member is leaving. And this charm offensive could prove hard to resist, since Scottish Government Ministers need influential allies in their fight to keep Scotland in Europe.

Indeed, given the political usefulness of this volte-face by European leaders and the fact that 62 per cent of Scots voted to Remain in the European Union rather than any other European destination, it might be difficult to sidle off stage left into a different trading relationship with EFTA. And yet, there is no point in Scotland not taking some time to take stock. As Jón Baldvin Hannibalsson points out, the EEA is a relatively stable group whilst the EU is probably facing a period of considerable change. Indeed EU Commission President Jean-Claude Juncker recently warned, there's every chance the EU may split up over Brexit.

---

7   Andrew Whitaker, 'Goodwill across Europe for Scotland in face of hard Brexit', *Sunday Herald*, 5 February 2017.

Who knows? But there's no point in deciding past political allegiances should automatically determine future ones.

It's interesting to note that relatively tiny and truly isolated nations like the Faroes, Greenland and Iceland seem to feel no need for the comfort, back-up or shelter the EU currently provides for most independence-seeking Scots. There's nothing sentimental about their decision not to become EU members – the importance of control over fishing effectively ruled membership out. There's also nothing modest – these truly tiny nations realise their own economic and strategic power and seem less anxious to have that validated and acknowledged by the great and good of Europe.

Has Scotland such smeddum?

Could an independent Scotland help steer the future direction of the European Union like Finland – away from the inflexible structures that suit big players and towards a diverse union that acknowledges the growing clout of small, asset-rich Baltic and North Atlantic players?

One of the arguments against EFTA is that the EU is making the rules of the single market, and EFTA members have to follow. If you are not in the EU, you do not have a seat at the table. Decisions are made without you. Also, while EFTA has no overarching political aims, it is in outlook dominated by free marketeering. There is no social component (like the EU's Social Chapter), and its ambition, as the name indicates, does not go beyond free trade.

The European Union, by contrast, is a much more ambitious project and one should not underestimate what the structural and cohesion funds have achieved in Scotland and Europe.

True, the EU's direction of travel since the 1980s, when Jacques Delors promoted a 'social Europe', has been towards a corporate, neoliberal project. And the Euro-crisis has certainly not added to its attractiveness. Yet, it is an organisation where, at present, 28 countries sit around tables, and share institutions, to resolve any problems arising. It has, without any doubt, contributed to decades of peace on a Continent that had plunged the world into two cataclysmic wars within one century.

And the EU is good at finding flexible solutions. In a joint article, David Martin MEP and Alyn Smith MEP cite, among others, the Faroe Islands, the Aland Islands and Heligoland as examples that demonstrate the variable geometry within Europe. None of their examples, they emphasise,

> provides a direct template for Scotland, the UK, nor anywhere else but they do illustrate the potential flexibility that exists and can be deployed to find answers that work. The EU can and does provide flexible solutions.[8]

This is backed by Professor Anton Muscatelli's who wrote in *The Sunday Times*: 'Europe, the European Economic area and the European Union are full of variable geometries designed to solve difficult economic and political issues affecting different territories, states and regions.'[9]

And some members, like Sweden see the EU as even more important now that the election of Donald Trump has thrown American support for political freedom and action against climate change into doubt.

In February, the Swedish Deputy Prime Minister posted a picture of herself signing a new Climate Change Act surrounded by female ministers – taking the mickey out of Donald Trump's much circulated photograph signing an

---

8   David Martin and Alyn Smith, 'Countries that show Scotland can stay in single market even after Brexit', *The Herald*, 7 February 2017.
9   Anton Muscatelli, 'We must calculate real cost of Brexit', *The Sunday Times*, 29 January 2017.

anti-abortion executive order, surrounded by men. Isabella Lövin said the Swedish government is 'the first feminist government in the world' and urged European countries to take over the climate change challenge as 'the US is not there anymore to lead'.

That's very significant. Swedes originally feared that the EU would act as an obstacle to their very equal way of life and social democratic path. Now they think the EU may be the only bulwark large enough to protect it.

Sweden has traditionally taken a totally different path to the USA, with a peaceful redistribution of political power and income during the 1930s that created the 'People's Home' – the world's most generous, effective and enduring welfare state. For this, the Swedes were openly criticised by successive American Presidents – indeed President Eisenhower envy-tinged remark about Sweden being a hotbed of 'sin, suicide, socialism and Smörgåsbord' was largely responsible for creating the unsubstantiated belief that Scandinavians are somehow morbid and depressed. All because the Swedish 'middle-way' of caring capitalism was producing a higher post war GDP than the USA. But under fire, the Swedes held firm. Half a century later, they are doing the same.

Today, Sweden accepts more refugees pro rata than any European country including Germany. They do have problems with integration, because few refugees arrive speaking Swedish in the way most arrive in Britain speaking some English and because the Swedes' regulated, high wage, high skills economy makes it hard for unskilled immigrants to get a job. But the Swedes are still committed to trying.

Which raises some interesting questions for Scots. Without trying to blindly copy anyone, it's easy to predict most Scots would rather resemble Isabella Lövin's feminist, climate-change-fighting Sweden than Donald Trump's protectionist, merciless America.

But do we feel more in common with Sweden and Finland working within the EU, or the North Atlantic fishing and energy states of Iceland and Norway, operating well outside it?

As we can see, the Nordic countries offer a veritable Smörgåsbord of relationships within and outwith the European Union, knitted together by a common Nordic cooperative outlook that created a common Nordic travel area (decades before Schengen) based on joint membership of the Nordic Council.

'There is a lot to be gained from being a small country in the EU,' Dominic Hinde argued at our 'Scotland after Brexit' conference: 'But we should perhaps not just take it for granted that EU membership is the only option.'

So let's have a serious discussion about the options open to Scotland. Maybe there's space for a dollop of haggis on the Nordic Smörgåsbord.

Nordic Country Profiles

Iceland

 Iceland was reputedly discovered by Irish monks before Ingólfur Arnarson decided to stay, arriving in Reykjavik in 874 AD. Thanks to the hostile conditions – a sub-Arctic climate, active volcanoes and piping hot geysers – there were no 'native' Icelanders for the young Norwegian settlers to supplant. The equal society set up in the remote, tiny state was run by the world's oldest extant parliament, Alþing, which met every year at Þingvellir – a striking venue at the heart of the island where the American and European tectonic plates are moving apart by around 2.5 centimetres every year. The settlers told fabulous stories of their predecessors in the Sagas – including raids on Ireland and the Scottish islands. To this day female Icelandic DNA is largely Celtic whilst male DNA is largely Nordic. The independent Icelanders reluctantly came under the control of Norway in 1262 after they lost all their trees – grazing and too much tree felling were to blame. When Norway in turn became the colonial property of Denmark, Iceland followed suit. But in 1944, Iceland declared full independence from Denmark. Despite recent volcanic eruptions and a financial crash that left the tiny population of Iceland almost bankrupt, the economy is recovering well based on education, geothermal energy, fishing and tourism. Iceland has the world's most literate population, the highest birth rate in Europe, the highest divorce rate, the highest percentage of women working outside the home, the highest male life expectancy, the happiest people (in 2008) and it's the only country in NATO without an army.

Norway

 Norway is a vast country stretching 1,500 miles from polar Svalbard in the north to Lindesnes lighthouse in the south. If you board a plane at Oslo, you'll reach Rome faster. Norway's rugged coastline is broken by thousands of islands and huge ice-gouged fjords – Sognefjord is the world's longest at 127 miles. Isolation and distance meant Norway was run by chieftains rather than a single King until Harald Fairhair (Harald Hårfagre) unified the country in 872. His harsh rule, according to the Sagas, prompted many Norwegians to leave as traders, Viking raiders and later settlers in Iceland, the Faroe Islands, Greenland, Orkney, Shetland, the Western Isles and Ireland. But since they built in perishable wood – the only tangible evidence of Norwegian presence in Scotland lies in DNA and island place names. Norway entered a union with Denmark and Sweden (then including Finland) when the Danish Queen Margaret became Queen of all three countries in 1397. Sweden later withdrew but Norway remained reluctantly until 1814 when control of Norway was handed to Sweden. Finally, Norway declared independence in 1905. There was no violence after a referendum found 368,208 supported the creation of a new Norwegian state with just 184 against. Norway was occupied by Germany during the Second World War and afterwards committed itself to peace-promoting policies abroad and equality at home. Norway struck oil in 1969 and opted to save the vast earnings in an Oil Fund – now the world's largest national pension fund. Norway is a very locally governed country with 429 tiny but powerful local councils. It has more wooden, weekend cabins than anywhere else in the world and took first place in the UN's Human Development Index (2013).

Sweden

Sweden, 14,000 years ago was covered by a thick ice cap. As the ice retreated, humans arrived. Sweden had a Viking Age (800–1050 AD) which saw plunder and trade along the Baltic coast and rivers stretching deep into Russia to the Black and Caspian Seas, where Swedes traded with the Byzantine Empire and Arab kingdoms. After breaking out of the Kalmar Union with Denmark, Gustav Vasa turned Sweden into a state (1523–60) In the 1600s that state became a Nordic super-state, controlling large parts of Denmark, Germany and Finland. But in the next century, Sweden lost most of these territories, surrendered Finland to Russia during the time of the Napoleonic Wars, but acquired Norway in 1814 until it became independent in 1905. One of the world's most comprehensive and generous welfare states (folkhemmet or People's Home) was put into effect after World War II. Modern Sweden is progressive, technologically advanced and green. It has one of the smallest pay gaps in the world between rich and poor workers, and excellent old folks care. It puts just one per cent of its waste to landfill and gets half its energy from renewable sources. The late Henning Mankell and Stieg Larsson have sold millions of books, 567 Nobel prizes have been won by Swedes and last year Swedes consumed 186,000 kilos of crayfish and 1,836,000 IKEA meatballs. Swedes publish statistics on almost everything and passed the world's first Freedom of Information Act. Sweden also welcomes proportionally more migrants than any European country except Germany.

Finland and Finnish Åland

 Finnish Åland is the only autonomous province in Finland with its own Government and powers over education, health, culture, industry and policing (though not taxation). The tiny electorate also elects a single representative to the Parliament in Helsinki. Åland got special exemption from EU tax regulations, when Finland joined in 1995. As a result, tourism and passenger ferries have thrived but local rights are protected. Incomers can only buy the most coveted coastal land after five years of residency. Ferries have a quota of spaces for locals, cyclists go free, not bikes or other vehicles, and rules require tourists to pay a higher fare if they drive across the islands to mainland without stopping overnight. Åland has been demilitarised since 1921, after the League of Nations settled the islands' future with an Autonomy Act in 1920. It exempted islanders from compulsory military service, guaranteed their right to learn and speak Swedish but kept them under the sovereignty of Finland which declared independence from Russia in 1917. During the Second World War, the Soviet Union demanded Finnish territory in Karelia. After this was rejected, Finland was attacked by the Soviet Union in the 'Winter War' of 1939. The Finns fought back successfully against overwhelming odds. Eventually, Finland was forced to give up Karelia. Finland's main export for decades were paper and pulp,

then Nokia phones and now chemical and machinery exports are important. In 2012, Finland spent more on research and development than any other European country, was Europe's most competitive region (and it's most remote) and regularly tops international league tables for school achievement.

Denmark, Greenland and The Faroe Islands

Denmark became the powerhouse of Scandinavia in 1397 when Danish Queen Margaret became the ruler of all Nordic nations. How did such a tiny nation manage that? Jutland is sandy and infertile and Copenhagen is built on an island. But Denmark's strategic position was the key to its success –guarding the Kattegat Strait which connects the North and Baltic Seas. The country lost its pole position after a series of disastrous military mistakes – the most recent depicted in unflinching detail by the recent BBC Four series 1864 – produced by the Danish Broadcasting Corporation which is also responsible for international hit series *Borgen*, *The Killing* and *The Bridge*. Modern Denmark is a very different story – characterised by social balance, equality, low levels of corruption and transparency. Danes pay high taxes but get affordable childcare, high minimum wages and high levels of unemployment benefit. Denmark has topped the EU's 'Eurobarometer' of wellbeing every year since 1973 and was recently ranked the happiest nation in the World Happiness Report. Around that time, when the oil crisis exposed Denmark's oil dependency, Danish politicians decided to keep the price of cars and petrol high. That's one reason around half of Danes commute to work and school by bike and Copenhagen has been judged the world's most ecologically friendly city, Denmark is on target to reach a goal of 50 per cent clean energy by 2020, and according to the Corruption Perceptions Index 2014, it's the world's least corrupt country. Greenland and the Faroe Islands are autonomous constituent countries within Denmark, each with their own parliament.

Luath Press Limited
committed to publishing well written books worth reading

LUATH PRESS takes its name from Robert Burns, whose little collie Luath (*Gael.,* swift or nimble) tripped up Jean Armour at a wedding and gave him the chance to speak to the woman who was to be his wife and the abiding love of his life. Burns called one of 'The Twa Dogs' Luath after Cuchullin's hunting dog in Ossian's *Fingal.* Luath Press was established in 1981 in the heart of Burns country, and now resides a few steps up the road from Burns' first lodgings on Edinburgh's Royal Mile. Luath offers you distinctive writing with a hint of unexpected pleasures.

Most bookshops in the UK, the US, Canada, Australia, New Zealand and parts of Europe either carry our books in stock or can order them for you. To order direct from us, please send a £sterling cheque, postal order, international money order or your credit card details (number, address of cardholder and expiry date) to us at the address below. Please add post and packing as follows: UK – £1.00 per delivery address; overseas surface mail – £2.50 per delivery address; overseas airmail – £3.50 for the first book to each delivery address, plus £1.00 for each additional book by airmail to the same address. If your order is a gift, we will happily enclose your card or message at no extra charge.

Luath Press Limited
543/2 Castlehill
The Royal Mile
Edinburgh EH1 2ND
Scotland

Telephone: 0131 225 4326 (24 hours)
email: sales@luath.co.uk
Website: www.luath.co.uk